Collins

11+ English

Quick Practice Tests
Ages 10-11
Book 3

Giles Clare

Contents

About this book	3	Test 16 Sentence Completion	42
Test 1 Comprehension	4	Test 17 Comprehension	44
Test 2 Spelling	8	Test 18 Spelling	48
Test 3 Punctuation	10	Test 19 Punctuation	50
Test 4 Sentence Completion	12	Test 20 Sentence Completion	52
Test 5 Comprehension	14	Test 21 Comprehension	54
Test 6 Spelling	18	Test 22 Spelling	58
Test 7 Punctuation	20	Test 23 Punctuation	60
Test 8 Sentence Completion	22	Test 24 Sentence Completion	62
Test 9 Comprehension	24	Test 25 Comprehension	64
Test 10 Spelling	28	Test 26 Spelling	67
Test 11 Punctuation	30	Test 27 Punctuation	69
Test 12 Sentence Completion	32	Test 28 Sentence Completion	71
Test 13 Comprehension	34	Test 29 Spelling	73
Test 14 Spelling	38	Answers	75
Test 15 Punctuation	40		

ACKNOWLEDGEMENTS

The author and publisher are grateful to the copyright holders for permission to use quoted materials and images.

Pages 4–5: Extract from *The Kid who came from Space* by Ross Welford. Reprinted by permission of HarperCollins*Publishers* Limited © 2020 Ross Welford.

Pages 14–15: Extract from *The Cracking Code Book* by Simon Singh. Reprinted by permission of HarperCollins*Publishers* Limited © 2004 Simon Singh.

Pages 24–25: Extract from *Darkmouth* by Shane Hegarty. Reprinted by permission of HarperCollins*Publishers* Limited © 2015 Shane Hegarty.

Pages 34–35: 'The Spider and the Fly' by Mary Howitt.

Pages 44–45: Extract from *The Time Machine* by H G Wells.

Pages 54–55: Extract from *Daddy-Long-Legs* by Jean Webster.

Pages 64–65: Extract from *Alice's Adventures in Wonderland* by Lewis Carroll.

Every effort has been made to trace copyright holders and obtain their permission for the use of copyright material. The author and publisher will gladly receive information enabling them to rectify any error or omission in subsequent editions. All facts are correct at time of going to press.

Published by Collins
An imprint of HarperCollins*Publishers* Limited
1 London Bridge Street
London SE1 9GF

HarperCollins*Publishers*
Macken House
39/40 Mayor Street Upper
Dublin 1, D01 C9W8, Ireland
ISBN: 978-0-00-876048-9
First published 2025
10 9 8 7 6 5 4 3 2 1

© HarperCollins*Publishers* Limited 2025

All rights reserved. No part of this publication may be reproduced, stored in a retrieval system, or transmitted, in any form or by any means, electronic, mechanical, photocopying, recording or otherwise, without the prior permission of Collins.

Without limiting the exclusive rights of any author, contributor or the publisher of this publication, any unauthorised use of this publication to train generative artificial intelligence (AI) technologies is expressly prohibited. HarperCollins also exercise their rights under Article 4(3) of the Digital Single Market Directive 2019/790 and expressly reserve this publication from the text and data mining exception.

British Library Cataloguing in Publication Data.

A CIP record of this book is available from the British Library.

Author: Giles Clare
Publisher: Clare Souza
Project Manager: Richard Toms
Editorial: Charlotte Christensen
Cover Design: Sarah Duxbury
Text and Page Design: Ian Wrigley
Layout and Artwork: QBS Learning
Production: Bethany Brohm
Printed in the United Kingdom by Martins the Printers

This book contains FSC™ certified paper and other controlled sources to ensure responsible forest management.

For more information visit: www.harpercollins.co.uk/green

About this book

Familiarisation with 11+ test-style questions is a critical step in preparing your child for the 11+ selection tests. This book gives children lots of opportunities to test themselves in short, manageable bursts, helping to build confidence and improve the chance of test success.

It contains 29 tests designed to develop key English skills.

- Each test is designed to be completed within a short amount of time. Frequent, short bursts of revision are found to be more productive than lengthier sessions.

- GL Assessment tests can be quite time-pressured so these practice tests will help your child become accustomed to this style of questioning.

- We recommend your child uses a pencil to complete the tests, so that they can rub out the answers and try again at a later date if necessary.

- Your child will need a pencil and a rubber to complete the tests as well as some spare paper for rough working. They will also need to be able to see a clock/watch and should have a quiet place in which to do the tests.

- Answers to every question are provided at the back of the book, with explanations given where appropriate.

- After completing the tests, your child should revisit their weaker areas and attempt to improve their scores and timings.

For more information about 11+ preparation and other practice resources available from Collins, go to our website at:

collins.co.uk/11plus

Comprehension

Test 1

You have 10 minutes to complete this test.

You have 10 questions to complete within the time given.

Read the text below and answer the questions that follow. In each question, circle the letter next to the correct answer.

EXAMPLE

Sam, an engineer from Liverpool, first met Lucy, a nurse from Chester, at a cricket club.

What was Lucy's occupation?

- **A** Engineer
- **B** Cricketer
- **(C)** Nurse
- **D** Doctor
- **E** Director

The following is an extract from *The Kid who came from Space* by Ross Welford

KIELDER, NORTHUMBERLAND
27 DECEMBER

Northumbria Police are seeking the public's help to find a twelve-year-old girl missing from Kielder Village, Northumberland, since Christmas Eve.

5 Tamara 'Tammy' Tait was last seen leaving her home near the Stargazer public house on a bicycle at around 6pm on 24 December.

She is described as white, around 160 cm tall, of medium build, with blonde hair and brown eyes. She was last seen wearing blue jeans and a red North Face branded puffer jacket.

Volunteer teams and police have spent two days searching the forests and moors surrounding
10 the remote village near the border between England and Scotland.

Anyone who may have seen Tamara or has any information in relation to her current whereabouts is urged to contact the police.

If you have information for the police, contact Policelink on 13 14 11 or call CrimeStoppers on 1800 333 000.

15 I read the sign again, glowing in front of me:

Type of organism: human female

Origin: Earth

Age: about twelve years

This brand-new exhibit will be introduced to the wider Earth Zone exhibition when emotional stability has been achieved

I looked at the bedraggled creature, and I wanted to reach through the unseen barrier and hold its hand. (This was neither allowed nor possible: the barrier would have repelled me with a painful shock.)

Its hair …

All right. I must stop saying 'it'. The sign says it is a female, and so it should be 'her' …

Her hair fell in tight twists. I should have liked to see it when it was clean. Her pale and hairless skin was dotted with darker spots ('freckles', they are called in her language). Her clothes were similar to those worn by the other humans in Earth Zone. She had trousers of a coarse-looking fabric and a thick-looking padded item of a lighter shade on top, while her feet were clad in big shoes fastened with looped cord.

Her face was dirty and streaked with tears, and her eyes shone wet and bloodshot. She had been weeping (this is normal – humans do it a lot), although the atomic-level mechanical medication that had been given to her had closed down a lot of her primary cognitive functions—

(Wait. Is this too complicated? Philip suggests I should write: 'Her brain had been made slow by the drugs she had been given.' And that is, I suppose, close enough. I shall let you decide.)

Despite this, there was a spark of life in her eyes. Perhaps the dosage was imperfectly calculated, or she had an ability to resist some of the medication.

Anyhow, she looked at me and I was struck by how very expressive human faces are.

She put her hand to her chest and for a brief moment I thought she was making the sign of the Hearters, but – obviously – she was not.

She looked at me intensely and said, 'Ta-mee.'

Just that: those two syllables.

She did it again: 'Ta-mee.'

I glanced over both of my shoulders, but nobody was watching as I held up my PG and recorded this bit. Communicating with the exhibits is not *exactly* prohibited, but nor is it encouraged.

Is that her name? I wondered.

I repeated the syllables she had said, although the sounds were hard for me to duplicate.

'Ta-mee,' I said.

She nodded her head and made a weird face, as though she wanted to laugh and cry at the same time, which I did not understand – and still do not, not fully. Human beings are strange.

I imitated her gesture, and said my name.

The human female tried to repeat it. It sounded nothing *at all* like my name. She tried again and got a little closer. I practised the sounds a couple of times, and then tried saying my name in a way she might be able to repeat.

'Helly-ann,' I said, and a slow smile formed on her mouth.

She blinked hard and said it back to me. I found myself smiling at her.

Then her smile faded and she said two more syllables. 'Ee-fan.'

A voice came from a speaker next to the sign: 'Your time is up. Move along. There is a queue of people behind you waiting to see the new exhibit. Do not take more than your allotted time. Next.'

① Where was Tammy last seen before she disappeared?

　A　In the Earth Zone exhibition
　B　On the moors in Scotland
　C　Near the Stargazer public house
　D　In a forest in Northumberland
　E　At a shopping centre in Kielder Village

② In which of these would you be most likely to come across the text given in the first section (lines 1–8)?

　A　A historical textbook
　B　A fantasy adventure novel
　C　A travel guide
　D　A script for a soap opera
　E　A social media post

③ What has happened to Tammy?

　A　She has been kidnapped and taken to Scotland.
　B　She has got lost on her way to work.
　C　She has run away from home and is hiding in a forest.
　D　She has been abducted and taken to an alien planet.
　E　She has been taken to a secret government facility.

④ 'This brand-new exhibit will be introduced to the wider Earth Zone exhibition when emotional stability has been achieved' (lines **19–20**)

What does this sentence suggest?

　A　Tammy is being prepared for release back to Earth.
　B　Tammy is too upset to be put on full display.
　C　Tammy is overexcited about going to the Earth Zone.
　D　Tammy is being studied before she is displayed.
　E　Tammy is going to be trained as a scientist.

⑤ *'Philip suggests I should write: "Her brain had been made slow by the drugs she had been given."'* (lines **34–35**)

Why does the writer include this sentence?

　A　To help the reader understand the complicated medical explanation that comes before it
　B　To introduce the reader to the character of Philip
　C　To warn the reader about how drugs can affect your brain
　D　To show that Tammy is being treated badly
　E　To show that the narrator comes from an advanced scientific world

6 In general, how does the narrator feel about Tammy?
  A The narrator is interested in but frightened of Tammy.
  B The narrator sees Tammy simply as a scientific specimen.
  C The narrator feels both curious about and sorry for Tammy.
  D The narrator is amused by Tammy's behaviour.
  E The narrator is distressed about what is happening to Tammy.

7 How does the writer make the reader feel sympathy for Tammy?
  A By making her completely different from the narrator
  B By focusing on what has happened to her clothing
  C By emphasising her sadness and isolation
  D By describing how Tammy will eventually be put in the Earth Zone
  E By showing that she cannot speak properly

8 What interrupts the communication between the narrator and Tammy?
  A An announcement tells the narrator to go.
  B A crowd enters the room.
  C The narrator is pushed aside by someone.
  D It is time for the Earth Zone exhibition to close.
  E Tammy is too sad to try to talk.

9 What type of words are the following? (line 47)
  repeated   said   were   duplicate
  A Adverbs
  B Conjunctions
  C Nouns
  D Prepositions
  E Verbs

10 Which of these words is a synonym for 'bedraggled'? (line 21)
  A Frightened
  B Untidy
  C Fresh
  D Dangerous
  E Imprisoned

Score: .... / 10

Test 2 — Spelling

You have 6 minutes to complete this test.

You have 12 questions to complete within the time given.

In each question, circle the letter below the group of words containing a spelling mistake.

If there is no mistake, circle the letter **N**.

EXAMPLE

He checked his calender twice to make sure he hadn't forgotten any important appointments.
A — (B) — C — D — N

1) Despite being strangers, the family was incredibly hospitible and welcomed us
   A — B — C
   with delicious, home-cooked meals.
   D — N

2) Her dedication and hard work made her a sucessful entrepreneur who built
   A — B — C
   a thriving business.
   D — N

3) The sun magicly appeared through the thick clouds just as we arrived
   A — B — C
   at the scenic viewpoint.
   D — N

4) She trained for months to prepare for the intense competition against some
   A — B — C
   of the world's best athletes.
   D — N

5. Reading and painting are my favourite passtimes, helping me to relax
   - A / B / C

   and express myself creatively.
   - D
   - N

6. The begining of the book was so intriguing that I couldn't stop reading until the very end.
   - A / B / C / D
   - N

7. The sudden interruption during assembly made it difficult for
   - A / B

   the children to stay focused on their performance.
   - C / D
   - N

8. He walked into the crowded hall, but he only recognised
   - A / B

   a few familiar faces from his school days.
   - C / D
   - N

9. Eager to catch the last bus of the night, he grabed his coat and ran along the wet pavement.
   - A / B / C / D
   - N

10. In a panic, she tried to decieve her classmates, but they quickly realised
    - A / B / C

    her story was fictitious.
    - D
    - N

11. The orcestra played a joyful symphony, filling the concert hall with
    - A / B / C

    a rich, harmonious sound.
    - D
    - N

12. My grandma's afternoon nap was disterbed by building work,
    - A / B

    making her grumpy for the remainder of the day.
    - C / D
    - N

Score: .... / 12

Punctuation

Test 3

You have 6 minutes to complete this test.

You have 12 questions to complete within the time given.

In each question, circle the letter below the group of words containing a punctuation mistake.

If there is no mistake, circle the letter **N**.

EXAMPLE

Just as the clock struck midnight there was a loud crash that echoed through the house.
  A   (B)   C   D   N

1. "I can't believe it!" said Leo. "You've found my missing notebook. Its been missing for weeks!"
   A   B   C   D   N

2. Despite being exhausted, Mia's little brother refused to sleep, he
   A   B

   wanted to hear another bedtime story.
   C   D   N

3. The mountain peaks encrusted in thick snow, glowed brilliantly under the moon's light.
   A   B   C   D   N

4. "We're finally here!" exclaimed Ethan. "After months of
   A   B

   planning, we've made it to the Grand canyon."
   C   D   N

5. The smell of buttery popcorn filled the air as Jasmine settled into her
   A   B   C

   seat and waited excitedly.
   D   N

6) In the field, the farmers sheepdog drove the scattered flock back towards the gate.
    [A]   [B]   [C]   [D]   [N]

7) "Your turn!" Ella said, handing the controller to her friend, Daisy. "Let's see if
    [A]   [B]   [C]

you can beat my score."
    [D]   [N]

8) I had three choices: Call for help, walk through the forest, or spend the night outside alone.
    [A]   [B]   [C]   [D]   [N]

9) The River Nile, winding through Egypt and Sudan, has been a source of life
    [A]   [B]   [C]

for thousands of years
    [D]   [N]

10) As the spaceship hovered over the surface of Mars,
    [A]   [B]

Commander Lee announced, "we're about to make history."
    [C]   [D]   [N]

11) After swimming in the pool for hours, I couldn't find my towel, so I borrowed my friend Joe's.
    [A]   [B]   [C]   [D]   [N]

12) The crumbling towers of the castle – abandoned many
    [A]   [B]

centuries ago cast long shadows over the valley.
    [C]   [D]   [N]

Score: .... / 12

Test 4: Sentence Completion

You have 6 minutes to complete this test.

You have 12 questions to complete within the time given.

In each question, circle the letter below the word or group of words that most accurately completes the sentence.

EXAMPLE

I have never [stand] [understanded] [stood] [understood] [understand] how the tides work.
           A   B   C   (D)   E

1. The goalkeeper was taken [aback] [down] [for] [off] [away] the pitch at half-time.
   A   B   C   D   E

2. After the battle, the soldiers returned to their [basis] [baize] [basses] [bass] [bases].
   A   B   C   D   E

3. My sister had [forgot] [forget] [forgotten] [forgetting] [forgets] her homework
   A   B   C   D   E

for the third time.

4. Harry had just had [the bad] [the worst] [worse] [the worse] [worst] day of his life.
   A   B   C   D   E

5. That painting won't look right [wherever] [whatever] [whomsoever]
   A   B   C

[whichever] [whoever] you put it up.
   D   E

6. If I had known you were ill, I [have] [should of] [had] [would have] [would]
   A   B   C   D   E

given you a hand.

7) The antidote should reduce the [affected] [effect] [infected] [affect] [effective]
   A B C D E

of the venom.

8) Our camping trip was so successful we are going [often] [today] [rarely] [never] [again]
   A B C D E

next week.

9) [Many] [Any] [Most] [Lesser] [Few] of an iceberg is hidden under the surface.
   A B C D E

10) The book [what] [where] [this] [that] [which] she borrowed from the library was
    A B C D E

extremely interesting.

11) The old cat [is lain] [was laying] [lied] [has lied] [had lain] on the warm
    A B C D E

windowsill all afternoon.

12) Our dog barked loudly [because] [so] [as well as] [whether] [just] it
    A B C D E

had seen a stranger near the house.

Score: .... / 12

Comprehension

Test 5

You have 10 minutes to complete this test.

You have 10 questions to complete within the time given.

Read the text below and answer the questions that follow. In each question, circle the letter next to the correct answer.

EXAMPLE

Sam, an engineer from Liverpool, first met Lucy, a nurse from Chester, at a cricket club.

What was Lucy's occupation?

- A Engineer
- B Cricketer
- **C Nurse**
- D Doctor
- E Director

The following is an extract from *The Cracking Code Book* by Simon Singh

On the morning of Saturday, October 15, 1586, Queen Mary entered the crowded courtroom at Fotheringhay Castle. Years of imprisonment and the onset of rheumatism had taken their toll, yet she remained dignified, composed and indisputably regal. Assisted by her physician, she made her way past the judges, officials and spectators, and approached the throne that stood
5 halfway along the long, narrow chamber. Mary had assumed that the throne was a gesture of respect towards her, but she was mistaken. The throne symbolized the absent Queen Elizabeth, Mary's enemy and prosecutor. Mary was gently guided away from the throne and towards the opposite side of the room, to the defendant's seat, a crimson velvet chair.

Mary Queen of Scots was on trial for treason. She had been accused of plotting to assassinate
10 Queen Elizabeth in order to take the English crown for herself. Sir Francis Walsingham, Elizabeth's principal secretary, had already arrested the other conspirators, extracted confessions and executed them. Now he planned to prove that Mary was at the heart of the plot, and was therefore equally to blame and equally deserving of death.

Walsingham knew that before he could have Mary executed, he would have to convince Queen
15 Elizabeth of her guilt. Although Elizabeth despised Mary, she had several reasons for being reluctant to see her put to death. Firstly, Mary was a Scottish queen, and many questioned whether an English court had the authority to execute a foreign head of state. Secondly, executing Mary might establish an awkward precedent – if the state is allowed to kill one queen, then perhaps rebels might have fewer reservations about killing another, namely
20 Elizabeth. Finally, Elizabeth and Mary were cousins, and their blood tie made Elizabeth all the more squeamish about ordering the execution. In short, Elizabeth would sanction Mary's execution only if Walsingham could prove beyond any hint of doubt that she had been part of the assassination plot.

The conspirators were a group of young English Catholic noblemen intent on removing Elizabeth, a Protestant, and replacing her with Mary, a fellow Catholic. It was apparent to the court that Mary was a figurehead for the conspirators, but it was not clear that she had given her blessing to the conspiracy. In fact, Mary *had* authorized the plot. The challenge for Walsingham was to demonstrate a clear link between Mary and the plotters.

On the morning of her trial, Mary sat alone in the dock, dressed in sorrowful black velvet. In cases of treason, the accused was forbidden counsel and was not permitted to call witnesses. Mary was not even allowed secretaries to help her prepare her case. However, her plight was not hopeless, because she had been careful to ensure that all her correspondence with the conspirators had been written in cipher. The cipher turned her words into a meaningless series of symbols, and Mary believed that even if Walsingham had captured the letters, he could have no idea of the meaning of the words within them. If their contents were a mystery, then the letters could not be used as evidence against her. However, this all depended on the assumption that her cipher had not been broken.

Unfortunately for Mary, Walsingham was not merely principal secretary, but also England's spymaster. He had intercepted Mary's letters to the plotters, and he knew exactly who might be capable of deciphering them. Thomas Phelippes was the nation's foremost expert on breaking codes, and for years he had been deciphering the messages of those who plotted against Queen Elizabeth, thereby providing the evidence needed to condemn them. If he could decipher the incriminating letters between Mary and the conspirators, then her death would be inevitable. On the other hand, if Mary's cipher was strong enough to conceal her secrets, then there was a chance that she might survive. Not for the first time, a life hung on the strength of a cipher.

1. Where did Mary Queen of Scots' trial take place?
    - **A** Windsor Castle
    - **B** The Tower of London
    - **C** Edinburgh Castle
    - **D** Fotheringhay Castle
    - **E** Hampton Court Palace

2. Why was Mary Queen of Scots on trial?
    - **A** For attempting to flee England
    - **B** For refusing to become a Protestant
    - **C** For plotting to assassinate Queen Elizabeth
    - **D** For being the Scottish Queen
    - **E** For executing her enemies

Questions continue on next page

(3) 'Mary was gently guided away from the throne and towards the opposite side of the room, to the defendant's seat, a crimson velvet chair.' (lines 7–8)

What does the empty throne in the courtroom symbolise?

- **A** Queen Mary's royal status
- **B** The power and authority of Queen Elizabeth
- **C** The fairness of the judges
- **D** The respect Elizabeth has for Mary
- **E** Mary's connection to her fellow conspirators

(4) How were Mary Queen of Scots and Queen Elizabeth related?

- **A** They were sisters.
- **B** They were cousins.
- **C** They were both queens.
- **D** They were both Catholic.
- **E** They were both Protestant.

(5) Why did Mary believe her letters could not be used against her?

- **A** She had written them in a foreign language.
- **B** She had never authorised the plot against Queen Elizabeth.
- **C** She destroyed all her letters before the trial.
- **D** She had used a cipher to encrypt their meaning.
- **E** She wrote her letters in invisible ink.

(6) What does the phrase 'establish a […] precedent' mean (line 18)?

- **A** To put a leader in power
- **B** To replace one ruler with another
- **C** To set a rule for the future
- **D** To plot against a leader
- **E** To prove something in a trial

(7) Who was Queen Elizabeth's principal secretary and spymaster?

- **A** Thomas Phelippes
- **B** Sir Walter Raleigh
- **C** Robert Dudley
- **D** Sir Francis Drake
- **E** Sir Francis Walsingham

8 What is the main point of the final paragraph?

- **A** Thomas Phelippes was an expert at breaking codes.
- **B** Ciphers are difficult for people to break.
- **C** The plot against Elizabeth was done through letters written in code.
- **D** Sir Francis Walsingham was good at finding evidence.
- **E** Mary's life depended on the quality of a secret code.

9 Which of these words is closest in meaning to 'onset' (line 2)?

- **A** Beginning
- **B** Creation
- **C** End
- **D** Birth
- **E** Raid

10 Which of these words is an antonym of 'squeamish' (line 21)?

- **A** Heroic
- **B** Nauseous
- **C** Comfortable
- **D** Timid
- **E** Shameless

Score: .... / 10

Test 6 — Spelling

You have 6 minutes to complete this test.
You have 12 questions to complete within the time given.

In each question, circle the letter below the group of words containing a spelling mistake.

If there is no mistake, circle the letter N.

EXAMPLE

He checked his calender twice to make sure he hadn't forgotten any important appointments.
   A   (B)   C   D   N

1) The temperature dropped so low overnight that the lake's surface was completely
         A   B   C
frozen by morning.
         D   N

2) Many people were moved to tears by the emotional speach my dad made
           A   B   C
at my sister's wedding.
         D   N

3) My little brother, who is an energetic toddler, is becomeing more confident
         A   B   C
at speaking every day.
         D   N

4) We couldn't bare the thick, purple carpets in our house when we first moved in.
         A   B   C   D   N

5) At summer camp, we went canoeing and surfing followed by archery,
         A   B   C
orienteering and absailing.
         D   N

18

6 She carefully cut the fabric into the perfect shape for her sewing project
   A   B   C

using sharp sissors and a template.
            D

7 That was definately the best spaghetti dish I have ever eaten, but the
         A   B   C

starter was a disappointment.
        D

8 The fireworks display created a stunning spectacal, lighting up the night
            A   B   C

sky with dazzling explosions.
        D

9 Our winter holiday, filled with adventure, laughter and a few disasters, was
         A   B   C

an unforgetable experience.
        D

10 The three siblings loved there new puppy and showered it with endless
          A   B   C

affection from the beginning.
        D

11 According to the weather forecast, it will rain heavily
           A   B

tomorrow afternoon, so we should bring umbrellas.
         C   D

12 As the sun rose the next morning, the birds were churping sweetly
         A   B   C

outside our bedroom window.
         D

Punctuation

Test 7

You have 6 minutes to complete this test.

You have 12 questions to complete within the time given.

In each question, circle the letter below the group of words containing a punctuation mistake.

If there is no mistake, circle the letter **N**.

EXAMPLE

Just as the clock struck midnight there was a loud crash that echoed through the house.
— A — (B) — C — D — [N]

1. At the skating rink, Ava twirled gracefully while her little brother wobbled
   — A — B — C —
   and nearly fell over
   — D —   [N]

2. As they hiked through Yosemite National park, Daniel said to
   — A — B —
   Gabriella, "Look at that eagle above the waterfall!"
   — C — D —   [N]

3. Outside Buckingham Palace, tourists gathered, hoping to see the
   — A — B —
   king or other members of the royal family.
   — C — D —   [N]

4. The ball flew past the goalkeeper. Ben shouted gleefully, "Goal! Thats three goals to nil."
   — A — B — C — D —   [N]

5. On Saturday mornings, Sanjay bakes fresh bread, the delicious aroma
   — A — B —
   wafts through the house and wakes everyone up.
   — C — D —   [N]

20

6 Ling grabbed her umbrella, sighed and muttered, "More rain.
   A — B
   That's just what I needed today."
   C — D

7 The instructions for the experiment were simple: mix the two
   A — B
   liquids observe the reaction and record your findings.
   C — D

8 "It's a disaster." said Dad, hunting around the picnic
   A — B
   table. "I think we've forgotten the ketchup."
   C — D

9 At the end of the weekend, the childrens' toys were all over the lounge,
   A — B — C
   kitchen, bathroom and stairs.
   D

10 Next Winter, we are planning a trip of a lifetime to visit the Great Wall of China.
   A — B — C — D

11 My grandma recently went to town to upgrade her old phone to a state-of the-art model.
   A — B — C — D

12 The next day, Lily carefully painted her wooden birdhouse,
   A — B
   adding tiny blue, flowers and green leaves.
   C — D

Score: .... / 12

Sentence Completion

Test 8

You have 6 minutes to complete this test.

You have 12 questions to complete within the time given.

In each question, circle the letter below the word or group of words that most accurately completes the sentence.

EXAMPLE

I have never | stand | understanded | stood | understood | understand | how the tides work.
   A   B   C   D (circled)   E

---

(1) After winning the final, we | going | is going | were gone | are going | gone |
                                   A   B   C   D   E

to celebrate in the clubhouse.

(2) Amy can be arrogant: she sometimes looks | forward to | down on | into | back to | for |
                                                  A   B   C   D   E

other people.

(3) Why do they always make me | were | we're | where | ware | wear |
                                  A   B   C   D   E

my brother's old clothes?

(4) Your grandparents' train | would have | could of | should be |
                                  A   B   C

| might of been | would have | arriving any minute.
       D   E

5) That umbrella is mine; the one over there must be [your] [her] [yours] [my] [their].
    A   B   C   D   E

6) Our hot air balloon floated [higher] [hire] [highest] [the highest] [hired]
    A   B   C   D   E

than the other one above the trees.

7) Maisie was sure her ring must be [everywhere] [where] [wherever]
    A   B   C

[somewhere] [whereas] in her bedroom.
    D   E

8) The garden of Fred's new house [backed down] [backs up] [backs off]
    A   B   C

[backed into] [backed onto] a car dealership.
    D   E

9) Shanice was determined to finish her project [whomever] [however] [forever]
    A   B   C

[whichever] [whenever] long it took.
    D   E

10) [Always] [Seldom] [Sometimes] [Yesterday] [Once] check that a campfire
    A   B   C   D   E

is out before you leave it.

11) The day [has begun] [beginning] [had begun] [begun] [is beginning]
    A   B   C   D   E

normally before the strange event took place.

12) Very [little] [more] [many] [few] [least] of the village remained after the
    A   B   C   D   E

devastating flash flood.

Score: .... / 12

Comprehension

Test 9

You have 10 minutes to complete this test.

You have 10 questions to complete within the time given.

Read the text below and answer the questions that follow. In each question, circle the letter next to the correct answer.

EXAMPLE

Sam, an engineer from Liverpool, first met Lucy, a nurse from Chester, at a cricket club.

What was Lucy's occupation?

A Engineer
B Cricketer
C Nurse
D Doctor
E Director

The following is an extract from *Darkmouth* by Shane Hegarty

From where its jutting, crooked horns met its great bull's head, it was covered in the mangy hair of a mongrel. As it looked back, slobber dripped from its great teeth and ran through the contours of muscles bulging along its back, past its waist down to patches of skin as cracked as baked clay. It stood on two legs that tapered down to menacing claws instead of hooves.

5   The Minotaur was worse than Finn had ever imagined it could be. And he had imagined it to be pretty bad.

It was looking straight at him.

He ducked into a doorway. A woman was already hiding there, her back pressed against the door, a dog pulled close. Her face was tight with fear.

10 "Don't worry, Mrs Bright," Finn told her, his voice muffled by the helmet. "You and Yappy will soon be safe, won't you, boy?" He petted the dog, a basset hound, with his free hand. It sneezed on him.

The woman nodded with unconvincing gratitude, then paused. "Where's your father, young man? Shouldn't he be—?"

15 There was a smash further up the street. The Minotaur had disappeared round the turn at the top of Broken Road. Finn took another deep breath and moved on after it.

From the other side of a wall, there was a thud so forceful it sent a shudder from Finn's feet to his brain, which interpreted it as a signal to run screaming in the opposite direction.

But Finn didn't run. He had trained for this. He had been born into it. He knew what was expected of him, what he needed to do. Besides, if he ran now, his dad would be disappointed in him. Again.

I'll be there when you need me, Finn's father had told him that morning.

Pressing a radio button on the side of his helmet, Finn whispered, "Dad? Are you there?"

The only response was the uncaring crackle of static.

A dark, looming hulk crossed an intersecting laneway, tearing along its narrow walls. Finn raised his Desiccator and followed. At the corner, he crouched and peered round. The Minotaur had paused no more than twenty metres away. Its great shoulders heaved under angry, growling breaths as it figured out which way to go next.

It was all up to Finn now. He recalled his training. Focused on what he had been taught. Thought about his father's expert words. Carefully, he aimed his stocky silver weapon, steadied himself, exhaled.

At that exact moment, the Minotaur turned to face him, its eyes like black pools gouged beneath scarred horns. Froth dripped from chipped and jagged tusks. For a second, Finn was distracted by the way drool, blood and rain clung to a crystal ring wedged through the Legend's nose.

The Minotaur roared. Finn squeezed the trigger.

The force of the shot sent Finn tripping backwards. A sparkling, spinning blue ball flew from the barrel of the Desiccator, unfurling into a glowing net as it was propelled towards where the Minotaur had stood only a moment before … and wrapped itself round a parked car.

Finn groaned.

With a flash and a stifled *whooop,* half the car collapsed in on itself with the anguished scrunch of a ton of metal being sucked into a shape no bigger than a soda can.

Finn looked for the Minotaur. It was gone.

He pressed his radio switch. "Erm, Dad?"

Still nothing.

He paused, calmed his babbling mind as much as he could and moved off again through the laneways. Using the ancient methods handed down to him, Finn began carefully tracking the trail of the Minotaur.

He needn't have bothered. The Minotaur got to him first.

1. What does the writer emphasise in the first paragraph?
   - A   The size of the Minotaur's teeth
   - B   The terrifying appearance of the Minotaur
   - C   How powerful the Minotaur is
   - D   That the Minotaur walks on two legs
   - E   That the Minotaur has poor skin and hair

2. 'The Minotaur was worse than Finn had ever imagined it could be. And he had imagined it to be pretty bad.' (lines 5–6)

   What do these sentences suggest about Finn's personality?
   - A   He is overconfident and underestimates the Minotaur's power.
   - B   He is easily scared and wants to run away.
   - C   He has a vivid imagination and a healthy sense of fear.
   - D   He is fearless and doesn't see the Minotaur as a threat.
   - E   He is confused and doesn't understand what he is up against.

3. Why does the writer include Mrs Bright and Yappy in the scene?
   - A   To show that Finn has other people helping him
   - B   To make Finn's mission more complicated
   - C   To show that other people do not trust Finn's abilities
   - D   To make Finn seem more heroic
   - E   To show that basset hounds make good pets

4. What is significant about Finn's father's silence on the radio?
   - A   It means his father is watching from a distance.
   - B   It shows that Finn's radio is broken.
   - C   It proves that Finn's father does not care about him.
   - D   It means that the Minotaur has already defeated Finn's father.
   - E   It means that Finn is alone in the fight for now.

5. What happens when Finn fires his weapon at the Minotaur?
   - A   It captures the Minotaur in a glowing net.
   - B   It shrinks a parked car.
   - C   It misses and explodes in the sky.
   - D   It knocks Finn over.
   - E   It creates a giant hole in the street.

6 What does Finn do after his first attack on the Minotaur fails?

- **A** He tracks the Minotaur through the laneways.
- **B** He runs away and hides.
- **C** He calls his dad for the first time.
- **D** He rescues Mrs Bright and her pet dog.
- **E** He reloads the Desiccator and chases the Minotaur.

7 Based on the whole text, what can you tell about Finn's relationship with his father?

- **A** His father is proud of him and supports him in everything he does.
- **B** Finn resents his father and doesn't want to follow in his footsteps.
- **C** His father doesn't care about Finn's successes or failures.
- **D** Finn looks up to his father but feels pressure to meet his expectations.
- **E** His father is no longer involved in his life.

8 What job do you think Finn and his dad do?

- **A** They are police dealing with strange cases.
- **B** They are scientists experimenting on mythical creatures.
- **C** They are monster hunters capturing legendary creatures.
- **D** They are archaeologists studying ancient myths.
- **E** They are treasure hunters searching for magical artefacts.

9 What type of words are the following? (line 1)

jutting   crooked   great   mangy

- **A** Conjunctions
- **B** Adverbs
- **C** Nouns
- **D** Adjectives
- **E** Pronouns

10 'At that exact moment, the Minotaur turned to face him, its eyes like black pools gouged beneath scarred horns.' (lines 32–33)

Which literary technique is used in this sentence?

- **A** Simile
- **B** Metaphor
- **C** Alliteration
- **D** Rhyme
- **E** Idiom

Test 10 — Spelling

You have 6 minutes to complete this test.

You have 12 questions to complete within the time given.

In each question, circle the letter below the group of words containing a spelling mistake.

If there is no mistake, circle the letter N.

EXAMPLE

He checked his | calender | twice to make sure he | hadn't forgotten | any important | appointments.
A — (B) — C — D — N

1. After hours of hiking, | they finally reached | the mountain peek, | where a breathtaking view awaited them.
A — B — C — D — N

2. A professional dietition | designed a meal plan | to help him improve his | health and fitness goals.
A — B — C — D — N

3. She signed up | for a cooking coarse | so that she could learn | interesting new recipes.
A — B — C — D — N

4. Their holiday was | full of new discoveries, | making it one of the most memorable trips | they had ever taken.
A — B — C — D — N

5. The next morning, | the bright, clear sky | and the fresh, cool air meant the | storm had finally past.
A — B — C — D — N

6. We had to cancel our picnic because of the torrencial rain that flooded the local park.
   A — B — C — D — N

7. The cricketer refused to give up on his dreams and remained fiercely determined despite
   A — B — C
   a series of injuries.
   D — N

8. It is neccessary to drink plenty of water daily to stay properly hydrated
   A — B — C
   and maintain good health.
   D — N

9. The huge forest was so dence with trees that sunlight barely reached the ground
   A — B — C
   through the branches.
   D — N

10. He giggled with embarrassment when he forgot his lines in front of the large audience.
    A — B — C — D — N

11. Ashamed that she had broken the priceless vase, she hesitated for a moment
    A — B — C
    before making her confesion.
    D — N

12. The new law about fossil fuels was contraversial, sparking heated debates among
    A — B — C
    politicians and citizens alike.
    D — N

Score: .... / 12

Punctuation

Test 11

You have 6 minutes to complete this test.

You have 12 questions to complete within the time given.

In each question, circle the letter below the group of words containing a punctuation mistake.

If there is no mistake, circle the letter **N**.

EXAMPLE

Just as the clock struck midnight there was a loud crash that echoed through the house.
  A   (B)   C   D   N

1. At the olympics in Paris, Clara went to see some athletics before visiting the Eiffel
        A   B   C
   Tower in the evening.
        D   N

2. "Let's build the biggest sandcastle ever!" shouted Oliver, grabbing his bucket and
            A   B   C
   running toward the wave's.
            D   N

3. Wasim, a retired accountant from Northampton sailed a yacht from Harwich to
         A   B   C
   Bergen in Norway.
        D   N

4. My sister-in-law was furious to discover she had been charged 125£ for parking
              A   B   C
   in the wrong place.
            D   N

5. "Disneyland Paris was magical," said Sophia. "However the queues
            A   B
   for rides were endless, which spoilt the experience."
            C   D   N

6) Dad said "I can't find my keys. I just had them a minute ago." He checked his pockets again.
   A   B   C   D   N

7) Under the shade of the oak tree, Mia read her favourite book and lost
   A   B   C
track of time completely.
   D   N

8) In Tokyo, Hiro checked his watch and said, "Mum's bullet train should
   A   B   C
arrive any second now."
   D   N

9) Marie Curie discovered radium and polonium – two radioactive
   A   B
elements earning her a Nobel Prize in 1903.
   C   D   N

10) "This puzzle's impossible!" groaned Leo, tossing another piece
   A   B
aside. "None of these pieces fit anywhere".
   C   D   N

11) Penicillin was discovered by accident in 1928 by Alexander Fleming,
   A   B
leading to the development of the first Antibiotics.
   C   D   N

12) Last Wednesday, I pushed my sister Zara higher and higher on the
   A   B   C
swings until she squealed.
   D   N

Score: .... / 12

Sentence Completion

Test 12

You have 6 minutes to complete this test.

You have 12 questions to complete within the time given.

In each question, circle the letter below the word or group of words that most accurately completes the sentence.

EXAMPLE

I have never | stand | understanded | stood | understood | understand | how the tides work.
               A   B   C   (D)   E

1) If only we | have | have had | had had | had have | having | a map with us,
            A   B   C   D   E

we wouldn't have got lost.

2) | They're | Their's | There's | Theirs | Their | is the house on the corner by the park.
   A   B   C   D   E

3) Alice was starting to fall | apart | behind | down | out | through | the others on the run.
                      A   B   C   D   E

4) The chef | paired | pears | pairs | pare | pared | off the rind with a peeler.
         A   B   C   D   E

5) Her smile was as bright | like | as | as if | as though | because | the morning sun.
                  A   B   C   D   E

6 Neptune is [further]A [father]B [far]C [the furthest]D [the further]E than Jupiter from the Sun.

7 I would leave that cat alone if I [was]A [am]B [had been]C [be]D [were]E you.

8 You will see that [big]A [small]B [large]C [little]D [tiny]E has changed since your last visit.

9 The janitor will see [through]A [off]B [to]C [in]D [red]E it that the gate is fixed immediately.

10 Next week, the class [went]A [gone]B [has gone]C [is going]D [going]E on a trip to the theatre.

11 The news about the school came as [whatever]A [somewhat]B [what]C [whatsoever]D [whatnot]E of a surprise.

12 I wish I had never [brought up]A [bought up]B [bringed up]C [brung up]D [buyed up]E the idea with you.

Score: .... / 12

Comprehension

Test **13**

You have 10 minutes to complete this test.

You have 10 questions to complete within the time given.

Read the text below and answer the questions that follow. In each question, circle the letter next to the correct answer.

EXAMPLE

Sam, an engineer from Liverpool, first met Lucy, a nurse from Chester, at a cricket club.

What was Lucy's occupation?

A Engineer
B Cricketer
(C) Nurse
D Doctor
E Director

The Spider and the Fly by Mary Howitt

"Will you walk into my parlour?" said the Spider to the Fly,
"'Tis the prettiest little parlour that ever you did spy;
The way into my parlour is up a winding stair,
And I have many curious things to shew when you are there."
5 "Oh no, no," said the little Fly, "to ask me is in vain,
For who goes up your winding stair can ne'er come down again."

"I'm sure you must be weary, dear, with soaring up so high;
Will you rest upon my little bed?" said the Spider to the Fly.
"There are pretty curtains drawn around; the sheets are fine and thin,
10 And if you like to rest awhile, I'll snugly tuck you in!"
"Oh no, no," said the little Fly, "for I've often heard it said,
They never, never wake again, who sleep upon your bed!"

Said the cunning Spider to the Fly, "Dear friend what can I do,
To prove the warm affection I've always felt for you?
15 I have within my pantry, good store of all that's nice;
I'm sure you're very welcome – will you please to take a slice?"
"Oh no, no," said the little Fly, "kind sir, that cannot be,
I've heard what's in your pantry, and I do not wish to see!"

"Sweet creature!" said the Spider, "you're witty and you're wise,
20 How handsome are your gauzy wings, how brilliant are your eyes!
I've a little looking-glass upon my parlour shelf,
If you'll step in one moment, dear, you shall behold yourself."
"I thank you, gentle sir," she said, "for what you're pleased to say,
And bidding you good morning now, I'll call another day."

25 The Spider turned him round about, and went into his den,
For well he knew the silly Fly would soon come back again:
So he wove a subtle web, in a little corner sly,
And set his table ready, to dine upon the Fly.
Then he came out to his door again, and merrily did sing,
30 "Come hither, hither, pretty Fly, with the pearl and silver wing;
Your robes are green and purple – there's a crest upon your head;
Your eyes are like the diamond bright, but mine are dull as lead!"

Alas, alas! how very soon this silly little Fly,
Hearing his wily, flattering words, came slowly flitting by;
35 With buzzing wings she hung aloft, then near and nearer drew,
Thinking only of her brilliant eyes, and green and purple hue –
Thinking only of her crested head – poor foolish thing! At last,
Up jumped the cunning Spider, and fiercely held her fast.
He dragged her up his winding stair, into his dismal den,
40 Within his little parlour – but she ne'er came out again!

And now dear little children, who may this story read,
To idle, silly flattering words, I pray you ne'er give heed:
Unto an evil counsellor, close heart and ear and eye,
And take a lesson from this tale, of the Spider and the Fly.

(1) How does the Spider first try to lure the Fly into his home?
- **A** To rest on a bed with fine sheets
- **B** To eat something nice in the pantry
- **C** To look in a mirror to admire herself
- **D** To see a pretty parlour full of interesting things
- **E** To escape from the thunderstorm

(2) What does the phrase 'who goes up your winding stair can ne'er come down again' (line 6) mean?
- **A** The Spider's home is a confusing maze for visitors.
- **B** Once inside, the Fly will be trapped and never escape.
- **C** The stairs are too steep to come back down safely.
- **D** The Fly cannot climb up the stairs.
- **E** The Spider has a magical staircase that disappears.

Questions continue on next page

3 Why does the Fly refuse to enter the Spider's pantry?

   A   She has heard that it is full of worrying things.

   B   She does not like the food the Spider is offering.

   C   She has recently eaten a big meal.

   D   She prefers to look for her own food.

   E   She does not like the colour of the curtains.

4 What does the phrase 'he wove a subtle web, in a little corner sly' (line 27) suggest about the Spider?

   A   He is worried about whether the Fly will come back.

   B   His is fixing his home while waiting for the Fly.

   C   He is building a home for the Fly.

   D   He is protecting himself against the Fly.

   E   He is carefully planning to trap the Fly when she returns.

5 What happens to the Fly in the end?

   A   She narrowly escapes and learns her lesson.

   B   She escapes but is hurt.

   C   She is caught and never seen again.

   D   She attacks the Spider and breaks the web.

   E   She tricks the Spider and flies away.

6 How does the Spider finally succeed in trapping the Fly?

   A   By using flattery to make her forget the danger

   B   By pretending to be injured and calling for help

   C   By convincing her that his home is safe

   D   By offering her a comfortable place to sleep

   E   By bullying her until she gives in

7 What is the tone of the final stanza?

   A   Humorous

   B   Light-hearted

   C   Cautionary

   D   Threatening

   E   Mysterious

8 What lesson is the poet trying to teach readers?

- **A** Avoid spiders as they are dangerous
- **B** Put your trust in people who say kind things to you
- **C** Look after flies because they are attractive
- **D** Ignore people who flatter or deceive you
- **E** Invite visitors into your home

9 Which of these is a synonym for 'wily' (line 34)?

- **A** Blunt
- **B** Honest
- **C** Slippery
- **D** Vague
- **E** Crafty

10 '"Will you walk into my parlour?" said the Spider to the Fly,' (line 1)

What literary technique is used in this line?

- **A** Alliteration
- **B** Personification
- **C** Simile
- **D** Repetition
- **E** Onomatopoeia

Score: .... / 10

Spelling

Test 14

You have 6 minutes to complete this test.

You have 12 questions to complete within the time given.

In each question, circle the letter below the group of words containing a spelling mistake.

If there is no mistake, circle the letter **N**.

EXAMPLE

He checked his | calender | twice to make sure he hadn't | forgotten any | important appointments.
A — (B) — C — D — N

1) He enjoyed sports | in general, but he was | particulaly passionate | about playing
   A — B — C

   basketball with his friends.
   D — N

2) Their description | of the suspect was | so detailed that | the police quickly
   A — B — C

   identified the person responsible.
   D — N

3) The farmer worked tirelessly | from sunrise to sunset, | plowing the fields | in preparation
   A — B — C

   for the new season.
   D — N

4) A giant chandelier | hung from the high cieling, | casting pretty patterns
   A — B — C

   across the grand ballroom.
   D — N

5. The original painting was displayed in the museum, while replicas were sold in the gift shop.
   A — B — C — D — N

6. A child ran across the park, laughing with joy as he released a bright red baloon into the sky.
   A — B — C — D — N

7. She tiptoed quitely into the room, careful not to disturb her sleeping baby sister.
   A — B — C — D — N

8. He speaks three different languages, which allows him to communicate easily when travelling abroad.
   A — B — C — D — N

9. When their car broke down in the middle of nowhere without a phone signal, their disasterous trip became worse.
   A — B — C — D — N

10. Even though the room was otherwise spotless, he noticed the tinyest specks of dust on the table.
    A — B — C — D — N

11. The marching band moved down the street, their drums booming and symbols crashing loudly in unison.
    A — B — C — D — N

12. To ensure a greener future for the next generation, the council's policies will focus on improving enviromental protections.
    A — B — C — D — N

Score: .... / 12

Punctuation

Test 15

You have 6 minutes to complete this test.

You have 12 questions to complete within the time given.

In each question, circle the letter below the group of words containing a punctuation mistake.

If there is no mistake, circle the letter N.

EXAMPLE

Just as the clock struck midnight there was a loud crash that echoed through the house.
A (B) C D N

1) In 1969, Neil Armstrong, the first human on the Moon, famously said, "that's one
   A   B   C
small step for a man."
   D   N

2) After hours of video games, Jamal stretched yawned and decided he needed a
   A   B   C
break and a snack.
   D   N

3) "Who wants popcorn?" Mum asked during movie night. She smiled as hands shot
   A   B   C
up around the room.
   D   N

4) Our family, dog Ross, wags his tail happily when he hears our kids returning from school.
          A   B   C   D   N

5. The Eiffel Tower, completed in 1889 for the Paris Exposition, was initially criticised for
   A — B — C
   its bold, modern design.
   D   N

6. My sister will only eat bland, processed food: I much prefer spicy, fragrant, colourful dishes.
   A — B — C — D   N

7. "Time for school!" Dad shouted. "Have you got your bags and lunchboxes?
   A — B — C
   What about your PE kits."
   D   N

8. The Wright brothers flew the first powered aeroplane in 1903 at Kitty
   A — B — C
   Hawk, north Carolina.
   D   N

9. "Whos ready for a board game?" asked my aunt. "If not, I've got some movies to watch."
   A — B — C — D   N

10. She offered the following explanation, the dog had stolen her homework and put
    A — B — C
    it in the washing machine.
    D   N

11. The Amazon Rainforest, located in South America, contributes significantly to the Earths
    A — B — C
    oxygen through photosynthesis.
    D   N

12. The strange noise coming from the dark corner of the room was nothing to fear or was it?
    A — B — C — D   N

Score: .... / 12

Sentence Completion

Test 16

You have 6 minutes to complete this test.
You have 12 questions to complete within the time given.

In each question, circle the letter below the word or group of words that most accurately completes the sentence.

EXAMPLE

I have never [stand] [understanded] [stood] [understood] [understand] how the tides work.
　　　　　　　A　　　　B　　　　　C　　　　(D)　　　　E

1. Miriam, [who] [whom] [whoever] [whose] [who's] I met last week, is in a rock band.
　　　　　　A　　B　　　C　　　　D　　　E

2. The detective was determined the thieves would not get [along with] [by] [on]
　　　　　　　　　　　　　　　　　　　　　　　　　　　　　A　　　　B　　C
[down] [away with] the coins.
　D　　　E

3. Our manager [deviced] [devise] [device] [devised] [is devicing] a new plan
　　　　　　　　A　　　　B　　　　C　　　　D　　　　E
to win the match.

4. The headteacher said, "Please explain what happened to your teacher and
[I] [me] [myself] [my] [your]."
A　B　　C　　　D　　E

5. A new piece by the composer [was sang] [is singing] [was sung]
　　　　　　　　　　　　　　　　A　　　　　B　　　　　C
[was singing] [has sung] by the choir.
　D　　　　　　E

42

6) Hasn't / Haven't / Isn't / Wasn't / Aren't we already seen this movie?
   A   B   C   D   E

7) It would be for better / good / the good / best / the best if you apologised for your mistake.
                  A   B   C   D   E

8) Tom has been bit / bite / bitten / biting / bites on his legs by mosquitoes.
                A   B   C   D   E

9) My sister asked if there were any more / anymore / much / less / fewest slices of cake left.
                                  A   B   C   D   E

10) While playing hide and seek, my friend coughed and gave back / in / up / away / way our position.
                                                                A   B   C   D   E

11) In bed, Maya read on to / on / onto / in / into the end of the chapter.
                      A   B   C   D   E

12) It was so many / so few / so much / so soon / so far colder today than yesterday.
            A   B   C   D   E

Score: .... / 12

Comprehension

Test 17

You have 10 minutes to complete this test.

You have 10 questions to complete within the time given.

Read the text below and answer the questions that follow. In each question, circle the letter next to the correct answer.

EXAMPLE

Sam, an engineer from Liverpool, first met Lucy, a nurse from Chester, at a cricket club.

What was Lucy's occupation?

- A Engineer
- B Cricketer
- **(C) Nurse**
- D Doctor
- E Director

The following is an extract from *The Time Machine* by H.G. Wells

The thing the Time Traveller held in his hand was a glittering metallic framework, scarcely larger than a small clock, and very delicately made. There was ivory in it, and some transparent crystalline substance. And now I must be explicit, for this that follows—unless his explanation is to be accepted—is an absolutely unaccountable thing. He took one of the small
5   octagonal tables that were scattered about the room, and set it in front of the fire, with two legs on the hearthrug. On this table he placed the mechanism. Then he drew up a chair, and sat down. The only other object on the table was a small shaded lamp, the bright light of which fell upon the model. There were also perhaps a dozen candles about, two in brass candlesticks upon the mantel and several in sconces, so that the room was brilliantly illuminated. I sat in a
10 low arm-chair nearest the fire, and I drew this forward so as to be almost between the Time Traveller and the fireplace. Filby sat behind him, looking over his shoulder. The Medical Man and the Provincial Mayor watched him in profile from the right, the Psychologist from the left. The Very Young Man stood behind the Psychologist. We were all on the alert. It appears incredible to me that any kind of trick, however subtly conceived and however adroitly done, could have
15 been played upon us under these conditions.

The Time Traveller looked at us, and then at the mechanism. "Well?" said the Psychologist.

"This little affair," said the Time Traveller, resting his elbows upon the table and pressing his hands together above the apparatus, "is only a model. It is my plan for a machine to travel through time. You will notice that it looks singularly askew, and that there is an odd twinkling
20 appearance about this bar, as though it was in some way unreal." He pointed to the part with his finger. "Also, here is one little white lever, and here is another."

The Medical Man got up out of his chair and peered into the thing. "It's beautifully made," he said.

"It took two years to make," retorted the Time Traveller. Then, when we had all imitated the
25 action of the Medical Man, he said: "Now I want you clearly to understand that this lever, being pressed over, sends the machine gliding into the future, and this other reverses the motion. This saddle represents the seat of a time traveller. Presently I am going to press the lever, and off the machine will go. It will vanish, pass into future Time, and disappear. Have a good look at the thing. Look at the table too, and satisfy yourselves there is no trickery. I don't want to
30 waste this model, and then be told I'm a quack."

There was a minute's pause perhaps. The Psychologist seemed about to speak to me, but changed his mind. Then the Time Traveller put forth his finger towards the lever. "No," he said suddenly. "Lend me your hand." And turning to the Psychologist, he took that individual's hand in his own and told him to put out his forefinger. So that it was the Psychologist himself who
35 sent forth the model Time Machine on its interminable voyage. We all saw the lever turn. I am absolutely certain there was no trickery. There was a breath of wind, and the lamp flame jumped. One of the candles on the mantel was blown out, and the little machine suddenly swung round, became indistinct, was seen as a ghost for a second perhaps, as an eddy of faintly glittering brass and ivory; and it was gone—vanished! Save for the lamp the table was bare.

(1) What object did the Time Traveller place on the table?
- **A** A small mechanical clock
- **B** Two brass candlesticks
- **C** A stack of old books
- **D** A model of a time machine
- **E** A small, shaded lamp

(2) Which materials was the Time Traveller's mechanism made from?
- **A** brass, wood, leather
- **B** metal, ivory, crystal
- **C** ivory, brass, fabric
- **D** leather, fabric, crystal
- **E** metal, glass, wax

Questions continue on next page

3) 'And now I must be explicit, for this that follows—unless his explanation is to be accepted—is an absolutely unaccountable thing.' (lines 3–4)

What does the narrator mean by this?

- A That he does not understand how the machine works
- B That the Time Traveller is tricking the observers with a clever illusion
- C That what happens next is a figment of his own imagination
- D That the Time Traveller is about to perform a dangerous experiment
- E That what happens next cannot be explained unless the Time Traveller is telling the truth

4) What does the detailed description of the lighting in the room suggest?

- A The Time Traveller wanted a dramatic atmosphere for his demonstration.
- B The model needs bright lighting in order to function.
- C The Time Traveller wants to show the observers that there is no trickery involved.
- D The narrator wants to describe a warm and cosy setting.
- E The candles are important for time travel.

5) What do all the observers do?

- A They touch the lever on the model.
- B They sit in chairs around the Time Traveller.
- C They ask the Time Traveller questions.
- D They inspect the model.
- E They laugh at the Time Traveller's explanation.

6) Who was the person who activated the model?

- A The Time Traveller
- B The Medical Man
- C The Psychologist
- D The Provincial Mayor
- E The Very Young Man

7) What happened when the machine's lever was turned?

- A A candle went out and the machine vanished.
- B The room became completely dark.
- C The octagonal table tipped over on the hearthrug.
- D The narrator collapsed in his armchair.
- E The candles fell off the mantel.

8 Why does the Time Traveller say to the Psychologist, "Lend me your hand." (line 33)?

- **A** The Psychologist has small fingers for the tiny lever.
- **B** The Time Traveller does not want to get his hands dirty.
- **C** The observers might think he is tricking them by touching the lever himself.
- **D** The Time Traveller is clumsy and does not want to break the model.
- **E** Filby is blocking the light so that he cannot see the lever clearly.

9 'On this table he placed the mechanism.' (line 6)

Which of these words is a preposition?

- **A** On
- **B** this
- **C** he
- **D** placed
- **E** mechanism

10 The voyage of the model Time Machine is described as 'interminable'.

Which of these words is closest in meaning to this description?

- **A** Boring
- **B** Endless
- **C** Long
- **D** Brief
- **E** Limited

Score: .... / 10

Spelling

Test 18

You have 6 minutes to complete this test.

You have 12 questions to complete within the time given.

In each question, circle the letter below the group of words containing a spelling mistake.

If there is no mistake, circle the letter **N**.

EXAMPLE

He checked his | calender | twice to make sure he hadn't | forgotten | any important | appointments.
A — (B) — C — D — N

1. It was difficult for crops | to survive because | the long drout had | left the soil dry | and cracked.
   A — B — C — D — N

2. He practiced the piano | for hours every day | to prepare for | his first concert | performance.
   A — B — C — D — N

3. His sudden appearance | at the party surprised | everyone since | they thought
   A — B — C
   he was out of town.
   D — N

4. To celebrate my grandfather's milestone birthday, | we managed | to fit exactly
   A — B — C
   eigty candles on his cake.
   D — N

5. Around his neck, the pirate | wore a golden medalion | that peeked out from behind
   A — B — C
   his long, scraggly beard.
   D — N

6 They found his arguments persuasieve, making it difficult for any of them to disagree
         A   B   C

with his point of view.
     D

7 After the accident at the skatepark, he needed several stiches on his forearm
       A   B   C

to close the wound.
     D

8 The lawyer presented clear evidence to prove that his client was innocent of all charges.
         A   B   C   D

9 She wore an elaborait costume, decorated with feathers, sequins and embroidery, for the
         A   B   C

grand masquerade ball.
     D

10 Since he was such a relaible team member, the teacher trusted him with the important
          A   B   C

task of captaining the team.
      D

11 The teacher asked the pupils to separate their desks before beginning the test activities.
         A   B   C   D

12 The skillfull artist painted a realistic portrait that captured every detail of
         A   B   C

her subject's likeness.
      D

Score: .... / 12

Punctuation

Test 19

You have 6 minutes to complete this test.

You have 12 questions to complete within the time given.

In each question, circle the letter below the group of words containing a punctuation mistake.

If there is no mistake, circle the letter **N**.

EXAMPLE

Just as the clock struck midnight there was a loud crash that echoed through the house.
A **(B)** C D N

1. Our cat, Rosie purrs and rubs against my trousers when I return home from school.
   A B C D N

2. The Great Wall of China, built over several dynasties, stretches about 13,000
   A B C
   Miles across northern China.
   D N

3. At the bus stop, Kasim said to his friend, "I hope we don't have another test today!
   A B C D N

4. "Lights out!" called Dad, but Jake kept reading he only had a few pages left.
   A B C D N

5. Next year, we are going to visit Tasmania in Australia to see the amazing Southern lights.
   A B C D N

6. "Let's go for a bike ride." suggested Amy. "It's a perfect day: warm and
      A   B   C
sunny with a breeze."
      D

7. As the storm raged outside, the family snuggled under warm blankets and
      A   B   C
watched a movie together.
      D

8. Did you know that Mount Everest is over 29,032 feet tall, making it the
      A   B   C
highest mountain on Earth.
      D

9. At the takeaway, Kyle ordered fizzy drinks, kebabs, sausages, chicken pies
      A   B   C
and fish, and chips.
      D

10. At the bowling alley, my sister in law picked the heaviest ball and fell over in the lane.
       A   B   C   D

11. "Hurry up!" shouted Poppy. "The movie starts in five minutes. Your going to miss the start."
         A   B   C   D

12. The Kingdom of Kush, an ancient African civilisation, built more pyramids
            A   B   C
than the Ancient Egyptians.
            D

Score: .... / 12

Sentence Completion

Test 20

You have 6 minutes to complete this test.

You have 12 questions to complete within the time given.

In each question, circle the letter below the word or group of words that most accurately completes the sentence.

EXAMPLE

I have never [stand] [understanded] [stood] [understood] [understand] how the tides work.
　　　　　　　　A　　　　B　　　　　C　　　　　(D)　　　　　E

1) We only ordered one pizza because two is always [to] [two] [much] [too] [more] much to eat.
　　　　　　　　　　　　　　　　　　　　　　　　　　A　　B　　　C　　D　　　E

2) I would have packed spare clothes if I [knew] [know] [had known] [is knowing] [knows] about the storm.
　　　　　　　　　　　　　　　　　　　　　　A　　　B　　　　C　　　　　D　　　　　E

3) They set off so [later] [late] [lately] [latest] [lateness] that they missed the show.
　　　　　　　　　　A　　　B　　　C　　　D　　　　E

4) Why are you disturbing me at [that] [those] [these] [the] [this] time of night?
　　　　　　　　　　　　　　　　　A　　　B　　　C　　　D　　　E

5) I used to jog every day, but now I [often] [soon] [always] [lately] [rarely] have the time.
　　　　　　　　　　　　　　　　　　　　A　　　B　　　C　　　　D　　　　E

52

6 Spring is my [personal]A [personnel]B [personally]C [person]D [personality]E favourite season of the year.

7 Our coach told us to do [ours]A [us]B [we]C [ourselves]D [our]E proud in the final.

8 The new café is the [popular]A [most popular]B [popularest]C [much more popular]D [so popular]E in the village now.

9 On our dream holiday, we [can't]A [should]B [had]C [might]D [could]E hardly believe what was happening.

10 A huge column of smoke [was rising]A [had rosed]B [rising]C [is risen]D [rosed]E from the volcano.

11 My cousin Sam is [in to]A [onto]B [on to]C [into]D [in]E hiking and climbing.

12 The sailors took shelter from the storm [aboard]A [under]B [below]C [above]D [on]E deck.

Score: .... / 12

Comprehension

Test 21

You have 10 minutes to complete this test.

You have 10 questions to complete within the time given.

Read the text below and answer the questions that follow. In each question, circle the letter next to the correct answer.

EXAMPLE

Sam, an engineer from Liverpool, first met Lucy, a nurse from Chester, at a cricket club.

What was Lucy's occupation?

- A Engineer
- B Cricketer
- **(C) Nurse**
- D Doctor
- E Director

The following is an extract from *Daddy-Long-Legs* by Jean Webster

10th October

Dear Daddy-Long-Legs,

Did you ever hear of Michael Angelo?

He was a famous artist who lived in Italy in the Middle Ages. Everybody in English Literature
5 seemed to know about him, and the whole class laughed because I thought he was an archangel. He sounds like an archangel, doesn't he? The trouble with college is that you are expected to know such a lot of things you've never learned. It's very embarrassing at times. But now, when the girls talk about things that I never heard of, I just keep still and look them up in the encyclopaedia.

10 I made an awful mistake the first day. Somebody mentioned Maurice Maeterlinck, and I asked if she was a Freshman. That joke has gone all over college. But anyway, I'm just as bright in class as any of the others—and brighter than some of them!

Do you care to know how I've furnished my room? It's a symphony in brown and yellow. The wall was tinted buff, and I've bought yellow denim curtains and cushions and a mahogany desk
15 (second hand for three dollars) and a rattan chair and a brown rug with an ink spot in the middle. I stand the chair over the spot.

The windows are up high; you can't look out from an ordinary seat. But I unscrewed the looking-glass from the back of the bureau, upholstered the top and moved it up against the window. It's just the right height for a window seat. You pull out the drawers like steps and walk
20 up. Very comfortable!

Sallie McBride helped me choose the things at the Senior auction. She has lived in a house all her life and knows about furnishing. You can't imagine what fun it is to shop and pay with a real five-dollar bill and get some change—when you've never had more than a few cents in your life. I assure you, Daddy dear, I do appreciate that allowance.

25 Sallie is the most entertaining person in the world—and Julia Rutledge Pendleton the least so. It's queer what a mixture the registrar can make in the matter of room-mates. Sallie thinks everything is funny—even flunking—and Julia is bored at everything. She never makes the slightest effort to be amiable. She believes that if you are a Pendleton, that fact alone admits you to heaven without any further examination. Julia and I were born to be enemies.

30 And now I suppose you've been waiting very impatiently to hear what I am learning?

I. Latin: Second Punic war. Hannibal and his forces pitched camp at Lake Trasimenus last night. They prepared an ambuscade for the Romans, and a battle took place at the fourth watch this morning. Romans in retreat.

II. French: 24 pages of the Three Musketeers and third conjugation, irregular verbs.

35 III. Geometry: Finished cylinders; now doing cones.

IV. English: Studying exposition. My style improves daily in clearness and brevity.

V. Physiology: Reached the digestive system. Bile and the pancreas next time.

Yours, on the way to being educated,

Jerusha Abbott

---

(1) Why did Jerusha's classmates laugh at her?

A She didn't know how to say Michelangelo's name.

B She didn't know who Hannibal was.

C She couldn't speak Italian.

D She got lost on her way to Geometry.

E She thought Michelangelo was an archangel.

(2) What point is Jerusha making in the first two paragraphs?

A She is fed up that other people laugh at her mistakes.

B She is cleverer than all the other girls.

C She does not know much about famous people.

D She is resilient when people laugh at her mistakes.

E She is not interested in her English Literature lessons.

Questions continue on next page

3 How did Jerusha solve the problem of the high window?

- **A** She decorated her room with second-hand furniture from an auction.
- **B** She stood on her mahogany desk.
- **C** She used an old bureau to create a window seat.
- **D** She tilted a mirror to see the reflection from outside.
- **E** She hid behind yellow denim curtains.

4 What does Jerusha's excitement about a five-dollar bill suggest?

- **A** She is careful with how she spends her money.
- **B** She didn't have much money before her allowance.
- **C** She enjoys getting a fair deal at the shops.
- **D** She is used to buying expensive furnishings.
- **E** She is wasteful with other people's money.

5 'She believes that if you are a Pendleton, that fact alone admits you to heaven without any further examination.' (lines 28–29)

What does Jerusha mean by this statement about Julia?

- **A** Julia thinks she doesn't need to prove herself.
- **B** Julia's background means she is rich and famous.
- **C** Julia had a religious upbringing.
- **D** Julia is bored by everything.
- **E** Julia laughs at Jerusha's mistakes.

6 Which of the following statements is false?

- **A** Jerusha finds Sallie McBride fun and entertaining.
- **B** Jerusha thought Maurice Maeterlinck was a freshman.
- **C** Jerusha uses a chair to hide an ink stain.
- **D** Jerusha is studying the Second Punic War in her Latin class.
- **E** Jerusha is ungrateful for the money she receives.

7 In which subject is Jerusha studying *The Three Musketeers*?

- **A** English Literature
- **B** French
- **C** Physiology
- **D** Latin
- **E** Geometry

8 What is the tone of Jerusha's letter?

   A Serious
   B Bitter
   C Light-hearted
   D Suspenseful
   E Apologetic

9 'He was a famous artist who lived in Italy in the Middle Ages.' (line 4)

   What type of word is 'who'?

   A Adjective
   B Verb
   C Common noun
   D Pronoun
   E Proper noun

10 'Do you care to know how I've furnished my room? It's a symphony in brown and yellow.' (line 13)

   Which literary technique is used in these sentences?

   A Alliteration
   B Simile
   C Metaphor
   D Rhyme
   E Personification

Spelling

Test 22

You have 6 minutes to complete this test.

You have 12 questions to complete within the time given.

In each question, circle the letter below the group of words containing a spelling mistake.

If there is no mistake, circle the letter **N**.

EXAMPLE

He checked his calender twice to make sure he hadn't forgotten any important appointments.
  A   (B)   C   D   N

1) To avoid hitting the deer that had unexpectedly run across the road,
      A   B   C

   the driver breaked suddenly.
              D   N

2) The path was lined by neat rose of tall flowers, all blooming in the summer warmth.
        A   B   C   D   N

3) The shop sells handbags, scarves, stylish jewellery pieces and a wide range of accesories.
        A   B   C   D   N

4) His curiosity about space meant he spent hours researching planets and galaxies online.
        A   B   C   D   N

5) She eagerly devoured the delicious desert, enjoying every bite of the rich, creamy cake.
        A   B   C   D   N

6. The ruins of the ancient temple stood on a tall mound surrounded by a dense tropical jungle. [N]
   A — B — C — D

7. My mum, who was a gymnast, is still so flexable that she can bend into astonishing shapes easily. [N]
   A — B — C — D

8. The tourists were warned that the brightly coloured frog was highly poisinous and should never be touched. [N]
   A — B — C — D

9. She packed warm clotheing in her suitcase as she knew that the mountain weather would be extremely cold. [N]
   A — B — C — D

10. At the airport, we struggled to carry all our heavy bagage while searching for the check-in counter. [N]
    A — B — C — D

11. The team became much stronger after the manager recriuted several highly skilled and experienced new players. [N]
    A — B — C — D

12. Our hotel's location was convenient, within walking distance of many restaurants and a variety of shops. [N]
    A — B — C — D

Score: .... / 12

Test 23 Punctuation

You have 6 minutes to complete this test.

You have 12 questions to complete within the time given.

In each question, circle the letter below the group of words containing a punctuation mistake.

If there is no mistake, circle the letter **N**.

EXAMPLE

Just as the clock struck midnight there was a loud crash that echoed through the house.
  A (B) C D N

1. The Ferris wheel at the funfair moved slowly, giving us a great view over the city.
   A B C D N

2. "One more game of tag!" begged my brother. "You wont catch me so easily this time."
   A B C D N

3. During our camping trip, Dad built a roaring fire that nearly set our neighbour's tent ablaze?
   A B C D N

4. Angel falls plunges nearly one kilometre from the top of a mountain
   A B C
   in Venezuela in South America.
   D N

5. Lucas kicked the football to Arthur, who scored an incredible goal from the half-way line.
   A B C D N

6 The Mayans and Aztecs used latex from the rubber tree to make
        A   B   C

waterproof shoes and containers.
        D   N

7 Ethan, who was sitting with his mum on a bench in the park spotted a baby rabbit.
    A   B   C   D   N

8 You mustn't forget to pick up Noah at six oclock from the drama workshop in town.
    A   B   C   D   N

9 Femi is reluctant to speak in class: She is worried other children will laugh at her ideas.
    A   B   C   D   N

10 "Can we go to the beach," asked George. "I want to build the biggest sandcastle ever."
    A   B   C   D   N

11 The Ishango Bone probably the oldest mathematical artifact in
        A   B

existence – was discovered in the Democratic Republic of Congo.
      C   D   N

12 Mr Baxter told the class, "I'm delighted with the quality of all of your homework projects.'
    A   B   C   D   N

Score: .... / 12

Sentence Completion

Test 24

You have 6 minutes to complete this test.

You have 12 questions to complete within the time given.

In each question, circle the letter below the word or group of words that most accurately completes the sentence.

EXAMPLE

I have never | stand | understanded | stood | understood | understand | how the tides work.
　　　　　　　　A　　　　B　　　　　C　　　　(D)　　　　E

1. I promise not to tell anyone your secret | but | since | whether | as much as | unless |
　　　　　　　　　　　　　　　　　　　　　　A　　B　　　C　　　　D　　　　　E

   you tell someone mine.

2. The burglar alarm | is rung | has been ringing | rings | have been rung | ringed |
　　　　　　　　　　　A　　　　B　　　　　　　　　C　　　D　　　　　　　E

   since six o'clock this morning.

3. Our neighbour, | whose | who | who's | whom | which | kind and friendly,
　　　　　　　　　A　　　B　　　C　　　D　　　E

   won a writing prize.

4. It is reported that | fewer | less | any | much | fewest | people are reading books.
　　　　　　　　　　　　A　　　B　　C　　D　　　E

5. Theo realised that he was different | than | too | as | from | at | his two brothers.
　　　　　　　　　　　　　　　　　　　　A　　　B　　C　　D　　　E

6) Amelia wished she [chose]A [had chosen]B [have chosen]C [chooses]D [choices]E a different starter at the restaurant.

7) It was time for the farmer to plough the field and [so]A [then]B [sew]C [when]D [sow]E the spring barley.

8) My penfriend, to whom I [writes]A [am writing]B [written]C [wrote]D [has written]E as a child, is coming to visit.

9) [While]A [As soon as]B [So]C [Besides]D [Yet]E the guests have gone, we need to get ready for our holiday.

10) Unfortunately, we [either]A [neither]B [nor]C [do]D [try to]E speak Spanish nor Portuguese.

11) The card says these flowers were [scent]A [scented]B [sent]C [cent]D [sending]E by your friends.

12) [Those]A [That]B [Them]C [This]D [Their]E are the trousers I've been telling you about.

Score: .... / 12

Comprehension

Test 25

You have 10 minutes to complete this test.

You have 10 questions to complete within the time given.

Read the text below and answer the questions that follow. In each question, circle the letter next to the correct answer.

EXAMPLE

Sam, an engineer from Liverpool, first met Lucy, a nurse from Chester, at a cricket club.

What was Lucy's occupation?

A Engineer   B Cricketer   C Nurse   D Doctor   E Director

The following is an extract from *Alice's Adventures in Wonderland* by Lewis Carroll

There was a table set out under a tree in front of the house, and the March Hare and the Hatter were having tea at it: a Dormouse was sitting between them, fast asleep, and the other two were using it as a cushion, resting their elbows on it, and talking over its head. "Very uncomfortable for the Dormouse," thought Alice; "only, as it's asleep, I suppose it doesn't mind."

5   The table was a large one, but the three were all crowded together at one corner of it: "No room! No room!" they cried out when they saw Alice coming. "There's *plenty* of room!" said Alice indignantly, and she sat down in a large arm-chair at one end of the table.

"Have some wine," the March Hare said in an encouraging tone.

Alice looked all round the table, but there was nothing on it but tea. "I don't see any wine,"
10 she remarked.

"There isn't any," said the March Hare.

"Then it wasn't very civil of you to offer it," said Alice angrily.

"It wasn't very civil of you to sit down without being invited," said the March Hare.

"I didn't know it was *your* table," said Alice; "it's laid for a great many more than three."

15 "Your hair wants cutting," said the Hatter. He had been looking at Alice for some time with great curiosity, and this was his first speech.

"You should learn not to make personal remarks," Alice said with some severity; "it's very rude."

The Hatter opened his eyes very wide on hearing this; but all he *said* was, "Why is a raven like a writing-desk?"

20 "Come, we shall have some fun now!" thought Alice. "I'm glad they've begun asking riddles.—I believe I can guess that," she added aloud.

"Do you mean that you think you can find out the answer to it?" said the March Hare.

"Exactly so," said Alice.

"Then you should say what you mean," the March Hare went on.

25 "I do," Alice hastily replied; "at least—at least I mean what I say—that's the same thing, you know."

"Not the same thing a bit!" said the Hatter. "You might just as well say that 'I see what I eat' is the same thing as 'I eat what I see'!"

"You might just as well say," added the March Hare, "that 'I like what I get' is the same thing as 'I get what I like'!"

30 "You might just as well say," added the Dormouse, who seemed to be talking in his sleep, "that 'I breathe when I sleep' is the same thing as 'I sleep when I breathe'!"

"It *is* the same thing with you," said the Hatter, and here the conversation dropped, and the party sat silent for a minute, while Alice thought over all she could remember about ravens and writing-desks, which wasn't much.

35 The Hatter was the first to break the silence. "What day of the month is it?" he said, turning to Alice: he had taken his watch out of his pocket, and was looking at it uneasily, shaking it every now and then, and holding it to his ear.

Alice considered a little, and then said, "The fourth."

"Two days wrong!" sighed the Hatter. "I told you butter wouldn't suit the works!" he added
40 looking angrily at the March Hare.

"It was the *best* butter," the March Hare meekly replied.

"Yes, but some crumbs must have got in as well," the Hatter grumbled: "you shouldn't have put it in with the bread-knife."

The March Hare took the watch and looked at it gloomily: then he dipped it into his cup of tea,
45 and looked at it again: but he could think of nothing better to say than his first remark, "It was the *best* butter, you know."

Alice had been looking over his shoulder with some curiosity. "What a funny watch!" she remarked. "It tells the day of the month, and doesn't tell what o'clock it is!"

"Why should it?" muttered the Hatter. "Does *your* watch tell you what year it is?"

---

(1) Who is asleep at the table?

- **A** The Hatter
- **B** The March Hare
- **C** The Dormouse
- **D** A raven
- **E** Alice

(2) What is strange about the table arrangement?

- **A** The table is small and cramped.
- **B** There are only enough teacups for three people.
- **C** The table is upside down.
- **D** There are cushions all over the surface of the table.
- **E** The table is large, but everyone is sitting in one corner.

(3) What does the Hatter mean when he says, "'Your hair wants cutting'"? (line 15)

- **A** He wants to give Alice a haircut himself.
- **B** He wants Alice to give him a haircut.
- **C** He is paying Alice a compliment about her hair.
- **D** He thinks Alice's hair is messy or too long.
- **E** He thinks his hair is shorter than her hair.

Questions continue on next page

4 How does Alice react to the Hatter's riddle at first?
- **A** She is worried that the riddle will be too difficult.
- **B** She is excited and thinks the riddle will be fun to solve.
- **C** She is disappointed because she already knows the answer.
- **D** She is annoyed as she doesn't like riddles.
- **E** She is confused and refuses to answer.

5 What is unusual about the Hatter's watch?
- **A** It tells the time backwards.
- **B** It tells the day of the month, not the time.
- **C** It works by using crumbs and butter.
- **D** It tells the month of the year, not the time.
- **E** It is set to the wrong year.

6 Which of the following statements about the text is false?
- **A** Alice is told there is no space at the table.
- **B** The Dormouse is used as a cushion at the table.
- **C** The March Hare dips the watch in a cup of tea.
- **D** The Hatter gives Alice a clear answer to his riddle.
- **E** The March Hare offers Alice some wine.

7 Thinking about the whole text, why do the March Hare and the Hatter tell Alice '"No room! No room!"' when she first approaches the table?
- **A** They enjoy nonsense and contradicting things that are true.
- **B** They are afraid that Alice will drink all the tea.
- **C** They like telling lies to strangers to upset them.
- **D** There is not enough space for her to join them at the table.
- **E** They want to keep Alice away because they are scared of her.

8 What is the writer trying to convey about the world Alice is in?
- **A** It is a strict world where everyone follows the rules.
- **B** It is a dangerous place full of danger.
- **C** It is a world where logic and reason do not apply.
- **D** It is a realistic world similar to the one Alice comes from.
- **E** It is a peaceful place where everyone enjoys interesting discussions.

9 What type of words are the following? (line 47)

Alice   shoulder   curiosity   watch

- **A** Adjectives
- **B** Adverbs
- **C** Verbs
- **D** Prepositions
- **E** Nouns

10 '"Yes, but some crumbs must have got in as well," the Hatter grumbled:' (line 42)

Which of these words is a conjunction?

- **A** Yes
- **B** but
- **C** some
- **D** got
- **E** the

Score: .... / 10

Spelling

Test 26

You have 6 minutes to complete this test.

You have 12 questions to complete within the time given.

In each question, circle the letter below the group of words containing a spelling mistake.

If there is no mistake, circle the letter **N**.

EXAMPLE

He checked his calender twice to make sure he hadn't forgotten any important appointments.
  A   (B)   C   D   N

1) The dancer's movements were graceful and rythmic, perfectly matching the beat and
          A   B   C
   style of the music.
          D   N

2) Every individual in our group played a vital role in making our presentation a success.
         A   B   C   D   N

3) She spent over forty minutes waiting in line before finally the shop opened its doors.
         A   B   C   D   N

4) The captain approached the referree, knowing that his decision could change the
              A   B   C
   outcome of the game.
          D   N

5) I spend hours studying the stars through my powerful telescope because I am
          A   B   C
   very intrested in astronomy.
          D   N

Questions continue on next page

6 She longed for a warm, sunny day as an escape from constant, misrable
              A   B   C

rain and gloomy skies.   [N]
   D

7 Until he apologised for the mistake he had made, his guilty conscience wouldn't let him rest. [N]
    A   B   C   D

8 It was a priviledge for the class to meet the famous author and discuss his latest book. [N]
    A   B   C   D

9 In deep space, the vacuum means that there is no air for sound to travel through. [N]
    A   B   C   D

10 After singing along for hours at the concert, her voice was horse and barely audible. [N]
    A   B   C   D

11 The politician launched a bold campain to clean up the sewage spills in the local river system. [N]
    A   B   C   D

12 Everyone was disappointed that the school fair was affected by a last-minute
          A   B   C

cancelation by the band.   [N]
     D

Score: .... / 12

Punctuation

Test 27

You have 6 minutes to complete this test.

You have 12 questions to complete within the time given.

In each question, circle the letter below the group of words containing a punctuation mistake.

If there is no mistake, circle the letter **N**.

EXAMPLE

Just as the clock struck midnight there was a loud crash that echoed through the house.
A (B) C D N

1. The Congo River is the second longest river in Africa. It's also the World's deepest river.
A B C D N

2. As the roller coaster reached the top Olivia clutched the safety bar and closed her eyes.
A B C D N

3. "Look, Mum! The penguins are waddling toward the water!" Said Lucas, pointing
A B C

excitedly at the pool.
D N

4. The Smith family were tired from their hike, they pitched their tent and
A B C

unrolled their sleeping bags.
D N

Questions continue on next page

5) On easter Monday, we are going to visit your grandparents' old house
   A   B   C

in the Scottish Highlands.
      D
N

6) "We won!" shouted Liam, throwing the ball in the air. "Thats three victories in a row!"
      A   B   C   D
N

7) At Times Square in New York, the honking of yellow taxis filled the cool night air.
         A   B   C   D
N

8) "The skatepark closes in an hour," said Max, grabbing his board. "We don't
        A   B   C

have time to waste"
       D
N

9) Tom adjusted his goggles, dived into the pool and kicked his legs. His big race had begun.
         A   B   C   D
N

10) We learned today that The Atacama Desert in Chile is one of the driest places on Earth.
         A   B   C   D
N

11) At the market, Leo helped his grandmother pick out some fresh apple's
        A   B   C

and some dainty cupcakes.
         D
N

12) Someone left these things outside a long hose, a pair of shears, a trowel and a lawn mower.
         A   B   C   D
N

Score: .... / 12

Test 28 — Sentence Completion

You have 6 minutes to complete this test.
You have 12 questions to complete within the time given.

In each question, circle the letter below the word or group of words that most accurately completes the sentence.

EXAMPLE

I have never | stand | understanded | stood | understood | understand | how the tides work.
           A   B   C   (D)   E

1) I | wasn't | daren't | doesn't | hasn't | weren't | tell my friend: she would be so disappointed.
   A   B   C   D   E

2) | Me and you | You and me | You and I | I and you | Me and me | are going on a surprise trip to the seaside.
   A   B   C   D   E

3) Sam was waiting all day for his cousin to come | after | under | up with | about | over |.
   A   B   C   D   E

4) " | Practised | Practice | Practiced | Practise | Practical | is important if you want to improve," said my guitar teacher.
   A   B   C   D   E

5) One of the | gooder | goodest | most better | best | more best | cities in Scandinavia is Oslo.
   A   B   C   D   E

Questions continue on next page

6 Before today, Arthur had never [flown]A [flowing]B [flew]C [flying]D [fly]E on an aircraft.

7 The general [poor]A [pours]B [pored]C [poured]D [pore]E over the map looking for

a place to rest.

8 "Is your purchase for [herself]A [ever]B [mine]C [yours]D [you]E or for a gift?"

the assistant asked.

9 My school has a system [whereas]A [whereby]B [somewhere]C [anywhere]D [wherever]E

pupils can earn merit points.

10 The suspect was seen making off [at]A [with]B [after]C [towards]D [in]E the

abandoned buildings.

11 Zainab would [much rather]A [much less]B [many more]C [anymore]D [rather much]E

play video games than watch television.

12 I should have [hanged]A [hanging]B [hang]C [hunged]D [hung]E the washing

on the line earlier.

Score: .... / 12

72

Test 29 — Spelling

You have 6 minutes to complete this test.

You have 12 questions to complete within the time given.

In each question, circle the letter below the group of words containing a spelling mistake.

If there is no mistake, circle the letter **N**.

EXAMPLE

He checked his calender twice to make sure he hadn't forgotten any important appointments.
A — (B) — C — D — N

1) The cheeky girl had a mischevious grin on her face as she hid her sister's favourite toy.
A — B — C — D — N

2) From the expedition camp in the valley, the mountains ahead looked impossibly
A — B — C
steep to climb over.
D — N

3) The loud construction noise became a newsance, making it extremely difficult for the
A — B — C
children to concentrate.
D — N

4) After hours of effort, he was delighted when he carefully inserted the final
A — B — C
peace of the puzzle.
D — N

Questions continue on next page

5) The army genral gave precise orders so that the soldiers could carry out
   A — B — C — their mission successfully. D — N

6) Our pet cat became aggressive when a stranger approached it and tried to stroke it.
   A — B — C — D — N

7) Between cereal and toast in the morning for breakfast, my prefrence has
   A — B — C — always been the latter. D — N

8) Walking around the city, it was impossible not to be impressed by the
   A — B — C — heights of the skyscrapers. D — N

9) The teacher's expression remained stirn, reminding the children that any nonsense
   A — B — C — would not be tolerated. D — N

10) She clumsily knocked over a large glass of milk, which soaked into the woollen carpet.
    A — B — C — D — N

11) Choosing to save money when I was young was the most sensibal decision I ever made.
    A — B — C — D — N

12) My brother's rude behaveyor during lunch embarrassed my parents in front of their guests.
    A — B — C — D — N

Score: .... / 12

Answers

Test 1 Comprehension

Q1 C *Near the Stargazer public house*
'Tamara 'Tammy' Tait was last seen leaving her home near the Stargazer public house'

Q2 E *A social media post*
The style of the first section is formal and factual. It can be inferred that such information and the plea for help would be posted on social media to reach as many people as possible.

Q3 D *She has been abducted and taken to an alien planet.*
Although aliens are not mentioned in the text, it can be inferred that Tammy has been taken to an alien planet and put on display in a sort of zoo that contains different species, including humans. For example, 'Her clothes were similar to those worn by the other humans in Earth Zone.'

Q4 B *Tammy is too upset to be put on full display.*
The phase 'when emotional stability has been achieved' suggests that Tammy is upset. She is not yet part of the 'wider Earth Zone exhibition', suggesting Tammy is being kept away from the main display.

Q5 A *To help the reader understand the complicated medical explanation that comes before it*
The explanation before is technical and complex: 'the atomic-level mechanical medication that had been given to her had closed down a lot of her primary cognitive functions'. It is most likely that the writer includes this simpler explanation to help the reader understand the meaning of the complicated one.

Q6 C *The narrator feels both curious about and sorry for Tammy.*
Evidence includes: 'I looked at the bedraggled creature, and I wanted to reach through the unseen barrier and hold its hand.' and 'Anyhow, she looked at me and I was struck by how very expressive human faces are.'

Q7 C *By emphasising her sadness and isolation*
Evidence includes: Tammy is behind an unseen barrier; she is dirty and she has been crying; she has been drugged to calm her down; she is trying to connect with the narrator.

Q8 A *An announcement tells the narrator to go.*
'A voice came from a speaker next to the sign: "Your time is up."'

Q9 E *Verbs*

Q10 B *Untidy*

Test 2 Spelling

Q1 C *hospitable*
Q2 B *successful*
Q3 A *magically*
Q4 N
Q5 B *pastimes*
Q6 A *beginning*
Q7 N
Q8 N
Q9 C *grabbed*
Q10 B *deceive*
Q11 A *orchestra*
Q12 B *disturbed*

Test 3 Punctuation

Q1 C *It's*
Q2 B *sleep. He* OR *sleep: he*
Q3 A *peaks, encrusted*
Q4 D *Canyon*
Q5 N
Q6 B *farmer's*
Q7 N
Q8 B *call*
Q9 D *years.*
Q10 C *"We're*
Q11 N
Q12 C *ago – cast*

Test 4 Sentence Completion

Q1 D *off*
Q2 E *bases*
Q3 C *forgotten*
Q4 B *the worst*
Q5 A *wherever*
Q6 D *would have*
Q7 B *effect*
Q8 E *again*
Q9 C *Most*
Q10 D *that*
Q11 E *had lain*
Q12 A *because*

Test 5 Comprehension

Q1 D *Fotheringhay Castle*
'On the morning of Saturday, October 15, 1586, Queen Mary entered the crowded courtroom at Fotheringhay Castle.'

Test 5 answers continue on next page

| Q2 | **C** | *For plotting to assassinate Queen Elizabeth* |

'Mary Queen of Scots was on trial for treason. She had been accused of plotting to assassinate Queen Elizabeth in order to take the English crown for herself.'

| Q3 | **B** | *The power and authority of Queen Elizabeth* |

'Mary had assumed that the throne was a gesture of respect towards her, but she was mistaken. The throne symbolized the absent Queen Elizabeth'

| Q4 | **B** | *They were cousins.* |

'Finally, Elizabeth and Mary were cousins, and their blood tie made Elizabeth all the more squeamish about ordering the execution.'

| Q5 | **D** | *She had used a cipher to encrypt their meaning.* |

'she had been careful to ensure that all her correspondence with the conspirators had been written in cipher.'

| Q6 | **C** | *To set a rule for the future* |

'if the state is allowed to kill one queen, then perhaps rebels might have fewer reservations about killing another'

| Q7 | **E** | *Sir Francis Walsingham* |

'Unfortunately for Mary, Walsingham was not merely principal secretary, but also England's spymaster.'

| Q8 | **E** | *Mary's life depended on the quality of a secret code.* |

'Not for the first time, a life hung on the strength of a cipher.'

| Q9 | **A** | *Beginning* |
| Q10 | **C** | *Comfortable* |

Test 6 Spelling

Q1	**N**	
Q2	**C**	*speech*
Q3	**C**	*becoming*
Q4	**A**	*bear*
Q5	**D**	*abseiling*
Q6	**D**	*scissors*
Q7	**A**	*definitely*
Q8	**B**	*spectacle*
Q9	**D**	*unforgettable*
Q10	**B**	*their*
Q11	**N**	
Q12	**C**	*chirping*

Test 7 Punctuation

Q1	**D**	*over.*
Q2	**B**	*Park*
Q3	**N**	
Q4	**C**	*That's*
Q5	**B**	*bread. The* OR *bread; the*
Q6	**N**	
Q7	**C**	*liquids, observe*
Q8	**A**	*disaster,* OR *disaster!*
Q9	**B**	*children's*
Q10	**A**	*winter*
Q11	**D**	*state-of-the-art*
Q12	**C**	*blue flowers*

Test 8 Sentence Completion

Q1	**D**	*are going*
Q2	**B**	*down on*
Q3	**E**	*wear*
Q4	**C**	*should be*
Q5	**C**	*yours*
Q6	**A**	*higher*
Q7	**D**	*somewhere*
Q8	**E**	*backed onto*
Q9	**B**	*however*
Q10	**A**	*Always*
Q11	**C**	*had begun*
Q12	**A**	*little*

Test 9 Comprehension

| Q1 | **B** | *The terrifying appearance of the Minotaur* |

The writer uses vivid imagery to describe the Minotaur's size, shape, strength and physical deformities to emphasise the creature's grotesque and frightening appearance.

| Q2 | **C** | *He has a vivid imagination and a healthy sense of fear.* |

Finn has used his imagination to picture how bad the Minotaur will be to prepare himself for what he will be up against.

| Q3 | **C** | *To show that other people do not trust Finn's abilities* |

'The woman nodded with unconvincing gratitude, then paused. "Where's your father, young man? Shouldn't he be—?"'

| Q4 | **E** | *It means that Finn is alone in the fight for now.* |

The text offers no evidence for any of the other statements, whereas it also states that Finn's father has told him that 'I'll be there when you need me'.

| Q5 | **B** | *It shrinks a parked car.* |

'With a flash and a stifled whooop, half the car collapsed in on itself with the anguished scrunch of a ton of metal being sucked into a shape no bigger than a soda can.'

| Q6 | **A** | *He tracks the Minotaur through the laneways.* |

'Finn began carefully tracking the trail of the Minotaur.'

| Q7 | **D** | *Finn looks up to his father but feels pressure to meet his expectations.* |

'Besides, if he ran now, his dad would be disappointed in him. Again.'

Q8 **C** They are monster hunters capturing legendary creatures.

Finn is tracking and attempting to capture the Minotaur using a specialised weapon. His father has trained him for this role.

Q9 **D** Adjectives
Q10 **A** Simile

Test 10 Spelling

Q1	C	peak
Q2	A	dietitian
Q3	B	course
Q4	N	
Q5	D	passed
Q6	C	torrential
Q7	N	
Q8	A	necessary
Q9	B	dense
Q10	N	
Q11	D	confession
Q12	B	controversial

Test 11 Punctuation

Q1	A	Olympics
Q2	D	waves
Q3	B	Northampton, sailed
Q4	C	£125
Q5	B	However,
Q6	A	said, OR said:
Q7	N	
Q8	N	
Q9	C	elements – earning
Q10	D	anywhere."
Q11	D	antibiotics
Q12	N	

Test 12 Sentence Completion

Q1	C	had had
Q2	D	Theirs
Q3	B	behind
Q4	E	pared
Q5	B	as
Q6	A	further
Q7	E	were
Q8	D	little
Q9	C	to

Q10 **D** is going
Q11 **B** somewhat
Q12 **A** brought up

Test 13 Comprehension

Q1 **D** To see a pretty parlour full of interesting things

"' 'Tis the prettiest little parlour that ever you did spy […] And I have many curious things to shew when you are there.'"

Q2 **B** Once inside, the Fly will be trapped and never escape.

It can be inferred that this phrase means that you can get in, but you cannot get out.

Q3 **A** She has heard that it is full of worrying things.

"'[…] I've heard what's in your pantry, and I do not wish to see!'"

Q4 **E** He is carefully planning to trap the Fly when she returns.

The poet uses the words 'subtle' and 'sly'. It can be inferred that this means that the Spider is carefully preparing a trap.

Q5 **C** She is caught and never seen again.

'He dragged her up his winding stair, into his dismal den,/Within his little parlour – but she ne'er came out again!'

Q6 **A** By using flattery to make her forget the danger

"'Come hither, hither, pretty Fly, with the pearl and silver wing;/Your robes are green and purple – there's a crest upon your head;/Your eyes are like the diamond bright, but mine are dull as lead!'"

Q7 **C** Cautionary

'To idle, silly flattering words, I pray you ne'er give heed:'

Q8 **D** Ignore people who flatter or deceive you

'Unto an evil counsellor, close heart and ear and eye,/And take a lesson from this tale, of the Spider and the Fly.'

Q9 **E** Crafty
Q10 **B** Personification

Test 14 Spelling

Q1	B	particularly
Q2	N	
Q3	C	ploughing
Q4	B	ceiling
Q5	N	
Q6	D	balloon
Q7	A	quietly
Q8	N	
Q9	D	disastrous
Q10	C	tiniest

Test 14 answers continue on next page

Q11 **C** cymbals
Q12 **D** environmental

Test 15 Punctuation

Q1 **C** said, "That's
Q2 **B** stretched, yawned
Q3 **N**
Q4 **A** family dog, Ross,
Q5 **N**
Q6 **C** food; I
Q7 **D** kits?"
Q8 **D** North
Q9 **A** "Who's
Q10 **B** explanation: the
Q11 **C** Earth's
Q12 **D** fear – or

Test 16 Sentence Completion

Q1 **B** whom
Q2 **E** away with
Q3 **D** devised
Q4 **B** me
Q5 **C** was sung
Q6 **B** Haven't
Q7 **E** the best
Q8 **C** bitten
Q9 **A** any more
Q10 **D** away
Q11 **A** on to
Q12 **C** so much

Test 17 Comprehension

Q1 **D** A model of a time machine

'On this table he placed the mechanism […] The only other object on the table was a small shaded lamp, the bright light of which fell upon the model.'

Q2 **B** metal, ivory, crystal

'[…] a glittering metallic framework […] There was ivory in it, and some transparent crystalline substance.'

Q3 **E** That what happens next cannot be explained unless the Time Traveller is telling the truth

'For that which follows […] is an absolutely unaccountable thing' means what happens next cannot be explained. The parenthesis '– unless his explanation is to be accepted –' is referring to the Time Traveller.

Q4 **C** The Time Traveller wants to show the observers that there is no trickery involved.

'It appears incredible to me that any kind of trick, however subtly conceived and however adroitly done, could have been played upon us under these conditions.'

Q5 **D** They inspect the model.

'The Medical Man got up out of his chair and peered into the thing. […] Then, when we had all imitated the action of the Medical Man […]'

Q6 **C** The Psychologist

'So that it was the Psychologist himself who sent forth the model Time Machine on its interminable voyage.'

Q7 **A** A candle went out and the machine vanished.

'One of the candles on the mantel was blown out, and the little machine […] vanished!'

Q8 **C** The observers might think he is tricking them by touching the lever himself.

This can be inferred from the context and the end of the previous paragraph: '"Look at the table too, and satisfy yourselves there is no trickery. I don't want to waste this model, and then be told I'm a quack."'

Q9 **A** On
Q10 **B** Endless

Test 18 Spelling

Q1 **C** drought
Q2 **A** practised
Q3 **N**
Q4 **D** eighty
Q5 **B** medallion
Q6 **B** persuasive
Q7 **C** stitches
Q8 **N**
Q9 **A** elaborate
Q10 **A** reliable
Q11 **N**
Q12 **A** skilful

Test 19 Punctuation

Q1 **A** Rosie, purrs
Q2 **D** miles
Q3 **D** today!"
Q4 **C** reading: he OR reading; he
Q5 **D** Lights
Q6 **B** ride,"
Q7 **N**
Q8 **D** Earth?
Q9 **D** fish and
Q10 **B** sister-in-law
Q11 **C** You're
Q12 **N**

Test 20 Sentence Completion

Q1	D	too
Q2	C	had known
Q3	B	late
Q4	E	this
Q5	E	rarely
Q6	A	personal
Q7	D	ourselves
Q8	B	most popular
Q9	E	could
Q10	A	was rising
Q11	D	into
Q12	C	below

Test 21 Comprehension

Q1   **E**   She thought Michelangelo was an archangel.
'[…] and the whole class laughed because I thought he was an archangel.'

Q2   **D**   She is resilient when people laugh at her mistakes.
'But now, when the girls talk about things that I never heard of, I just keep still and look them up in the encyclopaedia.' and 'That joke has gone all over college. But anyway, I'm just as bright in class as any of the others—and brighter than some of them!'

Q3   **C**   She used an old bureau to create a window seat.
'But I unscrewed the looking-glass from the back of the bureau, upholstered the top and moved it up against the window. It's just the right height for a window seat.'

Q4   **B**   She didn't have much money before her allowance.
'You can't imagine what fun it is to shop and pay with a real five-dollar bill and get some change—when you've never had more than a few cents in your life.'

Q5   **A**   Julia thinks she doesn't need to prove herself.
'[…] admits you to heaven without any further examination' suggests that Julia thinks her family name entitles her to lead a life where she does not need to prove herself through effort, kindness or achievement.

Q6   **E**   Jerusha is ungrateful for the money she receives.
'I assure you, Daddy dear, I do appreciate that allowance.'

Q7   **B**   French
'II. French: 24 pages of the Three Musketeers and third conjugation, irregular verbs.'

Q8   **C**   Light-hearted
Evidence includes: despite other people laughing at her mistakes, she doesn't seem to mind; she makes amusing observations about Julia.

Q9   **D**   Pronoun

Q10   **C**   Metaphor

Test 22 Spelling

Q1	D	braked
Q2	B	rows
Q3	D	accessories
Q4	N	
Q5	B	dessert
Q6	N	
Q7	B	flexible
Q8	C	poisonous
Q9	A	clothing
Q10	C	baggage
Q11	C	recruited
Q12	N	

Test 23 Punctuation

Q1	N	
Q2	C	won't
Q3	D	ablaze.
Q4	A	Angel Falls
Q5	D	halfway
Q6	N	
Q7	D	park,
Q8	C	o'clock
Q9	B	class: she
Q10	B	beach?"
Q11	A	Bone – probably
Q12	D	projects."

Test 24 Sentence Completion

Q1	E	unless
Q2	B	has been ringing
Q3	C	who's
Q4	A	fewer
Q5	D	from
Q6	B	had chosen
Q7	E	sow
Q8	D	wrote
Q9	B	As soon as
Q10	B	neither
Q11	C	sent
Q12	A	Those

Test 25 Comprehension

Q1   **C**   The Dormouse
'a Dormouse was sitting between them, fast asleep, and the other two were using it as a cushion'

Test 25 answers continue on next page

Q2	**E**	*The table is large, but everyone is sitting in one corner.*

'The table was a large one, but the three were all crowded together at one corner of it'

Q3	**D**	*He thinks Alice's hair is messy or too long.*

In this idiom, 'wants' means the same as 'needs'.

Q4	**B**	*She is excited and thinks the riddle will be fun to solve.*

"'Come, we shall have some fun now!" thought Alice. "I'm glad they've begun asking riddles."'

Q5	**B**	*It tells the day of the month, not the time.*

"'What a funny watch!" she remarked. "It tells the day of the month, and doesn't tell what o'clock it is!"'

Q6	**D**	*The Hatter gives Alice a clear answer to his riddle.*

The Hatter changes the subject without offering an answer: 'the party sat silent for a minute, while Alice thought over all she could remember about ravens and writing-desks, which wasn't much. The Hatter was the first to break the silence. "What day of the month is it?" he said'

Q7	**A**	*They enjoy nonsense and contradicting things that are true.*

There is lots of evidence throughout the text that the Hatter and the March Hare are contrary in nature and enjoy nonsense and wordplay. For example, "'Not the same thing a bit!" said the Hatter. "You might just as well say that 'I see what I eat' is the same thing as 'I eat what I see'!"'

Q8	**C**	*It is a world where logic and reason do not apply.*

The scene contains lots of examples of nonsensical, illogical behaviour, representing a world where ordinary rules are not followed. Examples include the table arrangement, the riddle without an answer and the Hatter's watch.

Q9	**E**	*Nouns*
Q10	**B**	*but*

Test 26 Spelling

Q1	**B**	*rhythmic*
Q2	**N**	
Q3	**N**	
Q4	**B**	*referee*
Q5	**D**	*interested*
Q6	**C**	*miserable*
Q7	**C**	*conscience*
Q8	**A**	*privilege*
Q9	**N**	
Q10	**C**	*hoarse*
Q11	**B**	*campaign*
Q12	**D**	*cancellation*

Test 27 Punctuation

Q1	**D**	*world's*
Q2	**B**	*top, Olivia*
Q3	**C**	*water!" said*
Q4	**B**	*hike. They OR hike; they*
Q5	**A**	*Easter*
Q6	**C**	*That's*
Q7	**N**	
Q8	**D**	*waste."*
Q9	**N**	
Q10	**B**	*the*
Q11	**C**	*apples*
Q12	**B**	*outside: a*

Test 28 Sentence Completion

Q1	**B**	*daren't*
Q2	**C**	*You and I*
Q3	**E**	*over*
Q4	**B**	*Practice*
Q5	**D**	*best*
Q6	**A**	*flown*
Q7	**C**	*pored*
Q8	**E**	*you*
Q9	**B**	*whereby*
Q10	**D**	*towards*
Q11	**A**	*much rather*
Q12	**E**	*hung*

Test 29 Spelling

Q1	**B**	*mischievous*
Q2	**C**	*impossibly*
Q3	**B**	*nuisance*
Q4	**D**	*piece*
Q5	**A**	*general*
Q6	**N**	
Q7	**C**	*preference*
Q8	**N**	
Q9	**B**	*stern*
Q10	**N**	
Q11	**C**	*sensible*
Q12	**A**	*behaviour*